The Ultimat Bread Machine Cookbook & Guide

Discover 100+ Easy and Delicious Bread Machine Recipes for Beginners to Make the Perfect Homemade Bread. With Tips and Techniques to Troubleshoot Common Issues and Elevate Your Bread-Making Skills to the Next Level!

Olivia Green

Legal Notice:

Copyright 2023 by Olivia Green - All rights reserved.

This document is geared towards providing exact and reliable information regarding the topic and issue covered. The publication is sold on the idea that the publisher is not required to render an accounting, officially permitted, or otherwise, qualified services. If advice is necessary, legal, or professional, a practiced individual in the profession should be ordered. From a Declaration of Principles which was accepted and approved equally by a Committee of the American Bar Association and a Committee of Publishers and Associations.

Disclaimer Notice:

The information herein is offered for informational purposes solely and is universal as so. The presentation of the information is without a contract or any type of guaranteed assurance. Readers acknowledge that the author is not engaging in the rendering of legal, financial, medical, or professional advice. Please consult a licensed professional before attempting any techniques outlined in this book. The trademarks that are used are without any consent, and the publication of the trademark is without permission or backing by the trademark owner. All trademarks and brands within this book are for clarifying purposes only and are the owned by the owners themselves, not affiliated with this document.

TABLE OF CONTENTS

INTRODUCTION 6

Benefits of Using a Bread Machine 7
Bread Making Explained in 5 Easy Steps 9
Tips on Saving Time When Cooking...11
Setting Up Your Bread Machine and Using Working Cycles Correctly.....................13
6 Common Mistakes Most Beginners Make 15
3 Bread Making Secrets to Make Bread Even More Delicious 17
How To Use Your Bread Machine in the Most Efficient Way 19

CHAPTER 1: FRUIT BREAD RECIPES.. 21

Strawberry Bread 21
Lemon Bread 22
Marzipan Cherry Bread 23
Lemon Raspberry Loaf 24
Blueberry Bread 25
Apple Chunk Bread 26
Banana Bread 27
Sweet Avocado Bread 28
Cranberry and Orange Bread...29
Citrus Bread... 30
Apricot Prune Bread 31
Raisin Bread 32
Raisin Candied Fruit Bread 33
Spice Peach Bread..34
Strawberry Oat Bread 35
Cocoa Date Bread...36
Fruit Syrup Bread 37
Chapter 2: Vegetable and Fruit Bread Recipes.. 38
Cauliflower and Garlic Bread.. 38
Zucchini Bread..39
Pumpkin and Sunflower Seed Bread 40
Carrot Bread 41
Almond Pumpkin Bread 42
Beetroot Bread..43
Tomato Bread 44
Orange Bread..45
Onion Bread... 46
Date Bread 47
Zucchini Herbed Bread...48
Plum Orange Bread..49
Keto Spinach Bread 50
Blueberry Oatmeal Bread 51
Red Bell Pepper Bread..52
Pineapple Coconut Bread...53
Flaxseed Bread 54

Orange Cranberry Bread 55
Broccoli and Cauliflower Bread 56
Celery Bread 57
Lemon-Lime Blueberry Bread 58
Potato Bread 59
Minted Bread 60
Apple Spice Bread 61
Coriander and Chili Bread 62
Peaches and Cream Bread 63

CHAPTER 3: BUNS AND BAGELS RECIPES 64

Onion Buns 64
Cottage Cheese Buns 65
Bacon Buns 66
Olive Buns 67
Lemon Buns 68
Whole-Grain Buns 69
Fig Rosemary Buns 70
Basil Buns 71
Healthy Whole-Grain Bagels 72
Sesame Savory Bagels 73
Cumin Bagels 75
Herb Savory Bagels 76
Chili Savory Bagels 77
Onion Bagels 78
Cheese Bagels 79
Herbed Buns 80
Apricot Bagels 81
Chocolate Bagels 82
Citrus Bagels 83
Raisin Bagels 84
Coconut Bagels 85
Nut Bagels 86

CHAPTER 4: KETO BREAD RECIPES 87

Yeast Bread 87
Keto Bread 88
Cream Cheese Bread 89
Almond flour bread 90
Cauliflower and Garlic Bread 91
Almond Meal Bread 92
Macadamia Nut Bread 93
Keto Breakfast Bread 94
Keto Sandwich Bread 95
Almond Flour Lemon Bread 96
Garlic, Herb and Cheese Bread 97
Cheesy Keto Sesame Bread 98

CHAPTER 5: HERBS AND SPICES BREAD RECIPES 99

Cajun Bread 99
Lavender Buttermilk Bread 100
Rosemary Bread 101
Chive Bread 102
Pumpkin Cinnamon Bread 103
Cinnamon Raisin Bread 104
Warm Spiced Pumpkin Bread 105

CHAPTER 6: GLUTEN-FREE BREADS 106

Chia Seeds Bread 106
Cherry-Blueberry Loaf 107
Saltless White Bread 108
Gluten-Free Whole Grain Bread 109
Gluten-Free Brown Bread 110
Raisin Bread 111
Oat Bread 112
Gluten-Free Chocolate Zucchini Bread 113
Cajun Veggie Loaf 114
Almond Butter Brownies 115
Low Carb Flax Bread 116
Bagels with Poppy Seeds 117
Parmesan Italian Bread 118
Nisu Bread 119
Nutty Cinnamon Bread 120
Gluten-Free Crusty Boule Bread 121

CONCLUSION 122

Introduction

If you love the idea of home baked bread but it just seems like a stretch too far with everything else you have going on, you might be wondering whether a bread machine could be the answer. There is nothing that compares with a fresh loaf of bread that's been made at home, and a bread machine might manage to make that a reality even if you have very little time to spare.

Indeed, baking bread at home could actually give you more time – because there's no need to pop to the shops to pick up a loaf of bread in time for breakfast or supper. You can have a fresh loaf on the go any time your stocks are getting low and you need a fresh loaf.

A lot of people love the idea of making their own bread, but there's no denying that this can be a pretty challenging thing to do. Bread making may not be enormously complicated, but it's time consuming; you have to spend a lot of time mixing, stirring, and then letting the dough prove, knocking it back, letting it prove again, and finally baking it. Unless you are at home for hours and you've got plenty of free time on your hands, this just isn't feasible, and that can be frustrating if you really love fresh bread and you want to make your own.

Fortunately, a bread machine is capable of doing all of this work for you, and some of the cleverest models can even add ingredients to the mix later on, meaning you literally just have to measure the ingredients and toss them into the machine.

The machine will then stir, combine, rest, prove, stir, and cook the dough, all according to the recipe that you have chosen. Bread machines can make all kinds of different loaves, and you can even whip up a dough in there and then bake it in the oven if you would prefer – which can be great for pizzas!

Bread machines automate pretty much the whole process, so you don't need to worry about setting the oven temperature, greasing the bread tins, checking on the loaf, or getting it out of the oven when the time is up. There's no risk of forgetting about it and burning it, which is great if you're juggling a lot of different tasks at once.

A bread machine might be one of the most useful gadgets you can have in your kitchen, and if you're short on time, it makes home baked bread accessible. You only need about five minutes to weigh and measure the ingredients out, and then you can set the timer and forget about it all until the smell of fresh bread begins to creep through the house and the alarm lets you know the bread is ready to be enjoyed. What could be better?

Benefits of Using a Bread Machine

There are quite a few benefits to using a bread machine, with the time saving being the most obvious and usually the biggest advantage. Let's explore why bread machines have become so popular in recent years.

Time Saving

We've already mentioned how the bread machine can turn a lengthy, complicated process that has many different steps to follow into something simple and straightforward that you can complete in a matter of minutes. The bread machine does all the work for you, and you still get an end product that is just as delicious as if you put the hours in yourself.

Delicious Bread

There's no doubt that bread bought in a shop will never compare with bread made at home. Shop-bought bread is full of preservatives, comes wrapped in plastic (usually), and is often far less tempting because it has to be made to last well, rather than made to maximise the flavour and texture. By contrast, homemade bread can be made with taste and texture at the forefront of its priorities, and you can also make it just the way you like it. Any time the last slice gets used up, you can just stick a fresh one on, and you'll have a loaf within a few hours.

Freezer Space

Even with modern preservatives, bread tends to have quite a short shelf life, and this can be frustrating. If you want bread for a week's worth of sandwiches, plus suppers and breakfasts, you will probably find that you have to shop multiple times per week. This adds a chore to your list and also often results in buying things that you don't want or need when you drop into the shop for bread. Some people get around this by putting an extra loaf of bread in the freezer, but bread is bulky to store, and this isn't ideal. If you can instead have a packet of flour and a bit of yeast in the pantry, you'll free up space in your freezer for more important products, and still have bread whenever you need it.

Flexibility

If anyone in your family has special dietary requirements, you'll probably find that bread is a major problem for them. Anyone who suffers from allergies will know the challenge of finding suitable foods, and staples like bread can be hard to get without allergens. Even if you can get them, they are often expensive to buy because they are considered speciality foods. However, with a bread maker, you can easily adjust your favourite recipe and you should soon have a loaf of bread that is suitable for the whole family to eat.

Energy Efficiency

Many people find that using a bread machine is more energy efficient than turning the oven on just to bake a loaf. This is particularly true if your kitchen is cold and you'd need the oven on low for proving the bread. A bread machine is a much smaller appliance, so it takes less energy to heat up and cook the bread.

This also frees your oven up for other cooking, so if you want to get dinner on the go, you won't have to wait for the bread to finish baking first.

Reduced Mess

Making bread by hand can be a pretty messy process. If you don't want flour all over your kitchen, a bread machine is the answer. For many recipes, you will only need the weighing scales, a measuring spoon, and a measuring jug for the water – everything else can be done in the bread pan. Even for more complicated recipes, you won't be flouring a surface to knead on, and this will massively reduce the mess.

Fewer Preservatives

If you don't like the idea of eating lots of preservatives or other unknown ingredients, shop-bought bread may not appeal to you enormously. However, homemade bread can be simplified to the very basic ingredients, and you'll always know exactly what you and your family are eating. This is vastly preferable for some people.

You can also reduce the amount of sugar and salt that you consume if you find recipes that depend on less of these two ingredients. Note that you shouldn't just cut them out entirely, though, or your bread may not rise properly.

No Kneading

One of the hardest parts about bread making is the kneading time. Although some people enjoy this, there's no denying that it is time-consuming and a bit of a chore, and without proper kneading, your bread won't have a pleasant texture. Fortunately, your bread machine will do all of this work for you, and to a very high standard. If you aren't a confident cook, this is an ideal way to ensure your bread turns out soft, fluffy, and delicious.

Bread Making Explained in 5 Easy Steps

There are five major steps to making bread – or at least, to making traditional bread like you might buy in a shop. These are all things that your bread maker will do for you, but it's well worth understanding what they are so you know how it's working.

Step One: Proofing the Yeast

This step is the first that your bread machine will do, and it happens after you have added all of the ingredients. However, if you are making bread by hand, you'll do it with just the sugar, yeast, and warm water. Sprinkle the yeast into the warm water and then stir in half a teaspoon of sugar and mix gently. The yeast will be activated by the water and will start to eat the sugar. After a few minutes, the mixture should turn frothy and then it will be ready to add to the dough.

Step Two: Making the Dough

Next, all of the ingredients need to be combined to start making the bread dough. If you are making bread by hand, this will involve mixing together the flour, salt, remaining sugar, yeast mixture, and usually a bit of oil or other fat. You'll need to mix hard to bring all of these ingredients together into a dough. Often, people reserve some of the flour and only mix it in once the dough has started coming together, as this makes it easier to mix. In your bread machine, the machine will use a metal paddle to mix the ingredients together, saving you a lot of hard work.

Step Three: Kneading the Dough

Once the dough is all mixed, you'll be kneading it, and for hand-made bread, this involves turning it out onto a floured surface and folding it over and over itself, rolling it back and forth, and generally improving its elasticity. This kneading process is a very particular technique, and it's crucial to making sure the texture of the bread works well.Kneading can be quite hard going, especially if you aren't used to doing it, and many amateur bakers find that they get tired before the bread is ready. When you are reasonably experienced, it should take about 5 to 10 minutes to properly knead a batch of dough, at which point it will be stretchy enough to see through without breaking. Again, a bread machine will do all of this work for you, kneading the dough to perfection with the paddle and incorporating both air and elasticity that will make the bread taste great.

Step Four: Allowing the Dough to Rise

Next comes the part that often takes the longest – the rising. You need to place your bread in a greased container with a clean towel across the top, and put it in a warm environment above 21 degrees C while the yeast does its work and the dough increases in size. It usually takes about an hour and a half for this rising process to finish, and the dough should approximately double in size.

At this point, your bread machine will go quiet and it will seem like nothing is happening. However, inside it, your bread will be nicely puffing up to fill the loaf tin, ready to be baked.

Step Five: Knock Back, Proof, and Bake

Once the dough has risen, you'll need to "knock it back," which involves punching some of the air out of it. It can then be transferred to the loaf tins, allowed to rise again for another 90 minutes, and baked. Most loaves are baked at about 190 degrees C for around 30 minutes, and then cooled on a wire rack for 10 minutes. The inside of the bread should reach a temperature of approximately 85 degrees C.

Your bread machine will once again handle all of this for you. There's no need to knock the dough back, grease tins, transfer the dough into the tins, or wait for it to rise again – this will happen automatically in the machine. It will then bake the loaf at the correct temperature for your recipe, and beep to let you know it's finished. As you can see, making bread in a machine can be a breeze!

Tips on Saving Time When Cooking

There are a few things that you can do to make cooking bread faster, whether you are using your machine or not. Let's explore them!

One: Use Bread Mixes

You can purchase bread mixes ready-made in shops, and these can be a massive time saver, although they do cost more than buying the ingredients individually. These bread mixes will have everything in them that is needed, except the water. Instead of having to weigh and measure the different ingredients, you can simply toss one of these in, add the water, and set the machine going. Most can also be used when baking by hand.

Two: Use a Timer

Some bread machine models have a timer option that lets you set the machine to bake when you aren't around, but even if your machine doesn't have one, you can use a manual timer switch. This will help to ensure that the bread is ready when you are at home to take it out of the machine, ensuring it can steam and cool properly – which often makes for better bread.

However, do remember that the yeast needs to be added at the right moment in order to work, so if your machine doesn't have a timed release switch for adding the yeast, this may not be possible. If you are at home and you want to put the ingredients in the machine and then add the yeast manually later, you can do this – just set an alarm so you don't forget to add the yeast.

Three: Make Your Own Mix

If you don't want to buy a ready-made bread mix, you can create your own mix in advance. Get some packets and weigh the ingredients out in batches. These can then be tossed into the bread machine at any time, without you having to get out the weighing scales every time.

Four: Slice and Freeze

Nothing beats fresh bread, but if you can't always make it or you don't use a loaf up quickly enough, consider slicing some and storing it in the freezer. This can be done with half loaves or full loaves. You don't have to slice it before freezing, but this makes it easier to just take out the slices you need and leave the rest.

Make sure you wrap the bread well if you are going to freeze it, because this will ensure that it doesn't get freezer burn or dry out. If you don't wrap the bread, it may turn crusty and crumbly in the freezer.

Setting Up Your Bread Machine and Using Working Cycles Correctly

You should always defer to the manual of your bread machine when setting it up and using the different cycles it offers, but here are a few tips that may help you to get to grips with it.

Your bread machine needs to be placed on a flat, heatproof surface. It will not get very hot in most cases, but may get warm, so a kitchen counter is a good spot. You will need a nearby plug socket that is not at risk of getting turned off mid-cycle.

Your bread machine has many different cycles, and it's worth looking through the manual to learn about them, as they can differ between machines. Some of the major cycles include:

- Kneading: this cycle mixes the ingredients together, and takes between 15 and 45 minutes. The paddle in the bottom of your bread pan will stir all the ingredients together. It may be worth checking that all of your ingredients are mixing in properly during this cycle.

- Rest: this is when your dough will start absorbing the liquid as the starch and gluten begin to react. Your bread machine will go quiet at this point and may not sound like it is doing anything.

- Rise: during this cycle, the dough will start proving, and should double in size. For many recipes, this takes around an hour, but don't be surprised if it's longer. Again, the machine will likely be quite quiet while the dough is rising.

- Punch: this cycle knocks the air out of the dough and helps to shape it. This cycle usually only lasts for a few seconds.

- Bake: in general, this takes between 30 and 90 minutes, but some loaves take longer. This is the point at which the machine will heat up, and the bread will actually cook. Once this has begun, you shouldn't open the lid of the machine, or you will let the heat out.

You can open the bread machine's lid through most of these cycles, but not during the baking cycle. If you need to make adjustments to the recipe, this should be done during the kneading cycle if possible.

Some people choose to only use the first few cycles and then remove the dough from the machine to shape and bake it in the oven. This works if you want baguettes, rolls, pizza bases, or other loaf shapes.

Knowing what cycle your bread machine is in can help if you need to check on your dough, add other ingredients, correct the moisture balance, shape the dough, remove the paddle, or take the dough out and bake it in your oven instead.

You should soon learn the different sounds that your machine makes as it progresses through the different cycles, and this will help you to establish whether you can open the top or not. Don't open the top once your bread is in its baking cycle, as this will release the heat and could prevent the bread from cooking properly.

6 Common Mistakes Most Beginners Make

It's always challenging when you first begin using a new gadget, so let's look at a few of the top mistakes you can avoid when you start making bread.

One: Leaving the Paddle in

One of the frustrating things about using a bread maker is that it leaves a large hole in the base of your nice, fresh loaf. This makes the bread harder to cut and spoils the appearance. It also makes the bread more difficult to use for sandwiches, because the bottom part of all the middle slices will have a chunk missing from it where the paddle was.

Fortunately, there's a simple fix. When your machine has finished pounding the dough and is about to start its baking cycle, open the lid of the machine, push the dough to the side, and remove the paddle. The dough can then bake as normal and you won't have a hole in your bread. This also negates the risk of the paddle getting stuck in the loaf, which can be very difficult to remove.

Two: Not Reshaping the Dough

If you've already opened the lid, it's well worth taking a bit of time to reshape the dough. You can shape it into a baguette, split it into rolls, or break it up into smaller loaves. Many people don't realise that this can be done when the machine has finished mixing, and it will make your bread machine a lot more flexible by allowing you to make many different shapes. If you want smaller loaves than your machine makes, it's a particularly good idea. You can still cook them in the machine if you want to, or you can take them out and put them in the oven.

Three: Using Hot Water

This is a mistake you should avoid whether you are using a bread machine or baking by hand. You need warm water, but not hot water, to activate the yeast. If you use hot water, the yeast will die, and the bread will fail to rise – because it's the yeast's activation that causes it to rise. The optimum water temperature is 38 degrees C, as this maximises the activation without harming the yeast.

Four: Adding Salt on Top of Yeast

If you put the salt directly on top of the yeast, it will kill it. You don't need to specifically separate the two ingredients, but make sure you aren't pouring the salt straight onto the yeast; mix them both with a little flour first. This ensures that the yeast doesn't get an enormous hit of salt, and it should then be fine.

Five: Cooling Your Bread at Room Temperature

Many people get the bread out of the machine and put it on the side in a cold kitchen, but this can lead to condensation that makes the top wrinkle and become crispy. To keep the top smooth and soft, take the loaf out of the pan and put it back in the warm bread machine with the lid propped open while it cools. In the warm machine, it will cool more slowly, and this makes for better bread overall.

Six: Adding the Ingredients in the Wrong Order

Did you know that you can put ingredients in the machine in the wrong order? This may not make a massive difference in some cases, but putting the liquids in your machine first is usually a better option. This stops the flour from puffing everywhere, and makes it easier to keep the yeast and salt separate. Add the yeast as the final ingredient for best results. It's worth checking this in your manual, in case the manufacturers recommend a different order, but if they don't, always go for wet ingredients first.

If you forget to do this, don't panic – your bread should still come out okay as long as the salt hasn't ruined the yeast. However, the texture may not be quite as pleasant, so it's good to get into the habit of following a particular order for adding your ingredients.

3 Bread Making Secrets to Make Bread Even More Delicious

Now you know what actions to avoid, let's look at what you should do to make your bread amazing.

Tip One: Measure Ingredients Carefully

If you're used to eyeballing your recipes – stop doing so. Precise measuring will make your bread great. Make sure you are using a digital scale for the best results, because even a little too much flour, salt, or sugar could ruin your bread and make it taste funny. If you aren't using scales, make sure you are levelling off your measuring cups so you don't have extra amounts of any ingredient.

If you are going to measure out packets of bread mix in advance, make sure you are particularly vigilant about using a proper set of scales. If you don't already have digital scales, it may be worth investing in a pair, as this will increase the accuracy of your bread making – and improve the results.

Tip Two: Use Room Temperature Ingredients

Because you are adding warm water to activate the yeast, you already know you want your recipe to be warm (although not hot). That means you shouldn't add cold ingredients if you can avoid it. If your recipe calls for milk, eggs, or butter, let these ingredients sit on the counter for a while before you add them to the bread machine. This might feel annoying, but it shouldn't take long, and it can make a surprising difference to the outcome.

If you add cold ingredients, you will bring the overall temperature of the dough down, and this will make the yeast work more slowly. If you are making bread by hand, you can just add a little time to the proving period, but in a bread machine, this can be complicated because the times are pre-set. It is therefore well worth making sure your ingredients are at room temperature, rather than cold, before you add them to your recipe.

Tip Three: Let the Bread Cool

Most people find it hard to resist warm bread; the first thing they want to do is cut it open when it comes out of the oven – which is a mistake. Warm bread definitely smells good, but you should still allow it to cool before you cut it. There are a couple of reasons for this.

The first is that freshly baked bread is still actually baking inside when it comes out of the oven or bread maker. It won't have any visibly raw dough, but the ingredients are still cooking a little, and the texture will be better if you let them finish before you cut the bread. Bread that is cut too soon may be too soggy inside.

Secondly, fresh bread is very hard to cut, which could result in a squashed, unappealing loaf with uneven slices. Even if you have an automatic slicing machine, it can be really hard to cut fresh bread properly, so it's well worth giving it a bit of time to cool, firm up, and release its steam.

Within about 30 minutes, it should have completely stopped cooking, and ought to be cool enough to slice. If you leave it to cool in the oven or bread maker, it may take a bit longer to reach a good slicing temperature.

How To Use Your Bread Machine in the Most Efficient Way

Finally, let's look at how you can maximise the efficiency of your bread machine so it serves you well.

Tip One: Run it at Night

If you are on a low energy tariff, you may find that your bread machine is much cheaper to run if you use a timer to make use of it overnight. Many of the recipes that take a long time also make really good bread, so if you can set the machine going before you go to bed at night, you'll have a fresh, hot loaf ready for the morning. You may also pay less in terms of electricity if you have this sort of contract set up with your energy company.

It's always worth running gadgets at night if you can, as this avoids having a lot of noise and heat in your kitchen, and reduces the risk of something getting interrupted by somebody accidentally unplugging it. Many of your gadgets can be run overnight if you use timers or long programs, and a lot of people say that the bread machine's longer cooking times actually make much better bread – so give this a try.

Tip Two: Use the Right Yeast

If you look closely at the packaging of your yeast, you'll see whether it says it is intended for hand baking or use in a bread machine. Using the right kind of yeast is important, because a bread machine does have set times for rising and proving. You can get instant yeast or rapid rise yeast, and if you buy rapid rise, you can use the rapid bake cycle on your bread machine and may be able to get good bread ready in under an hour.

Some people don't like the taste of bread made using rapid rise yeast as much, because there is less time for its flavours to meld and develop, but this is a great option if you need bread in a hurry. Don't use yeast that needs to be activated in advance in a bread machine if you can avoid it, because it may not sync up with your machine's cycles, and this will stop your bread from rising as it should.

Tip Three: Learn Your Flour

Bread comes out much better if you use the appropriate flour. You can purchase bread flour from most supermarkets, and as the name suggests, this will work well for baking loaves. Bread flour (or strong flour) contains a lot of gluten, which will help it to make super fluffy, elasticy bread that tastes great and lasts well. If you can't get strong flour or bread flour, plain flour will still work, but you will find that the bread isn't as appealing.

You can add other kinds of flour to your bread maker too, including wholemeal flour, rye flour, buckwheat flour, and more. These will all change the taste and texture of your bread, so it's worth experimenting and finding out which ones work for you. To minimise waste, always use a recipe or try out small loaves before you make big batches using different flour ratios.

Tip Four: Check the "Extras" Settings

Different bread machines will have different settings, and the higher quality your machine is, the more likely it is to have settings you can play around with. For example, some bread machines will let you adjust how dark the crust of your bread is, and some will have a slot you can add other ingredients to. The slot will then drop these into the dough at the appropriate time and the paddle will mix them in.

This is great if you want sunflower seeds, chopped nuts, sundried tomatoes, fruit, or olives in your bread, as these cannot be added until the bread has been kneaded. If your machine has one of these slots, make sure you are utilising it to maximise your efficiency and try out different recipe options.

Tip Five: Use its Mixing Cycles

If you are making other dough products, remember that you can use your bread machine to do all the hard work of mixing, kneading, and proving for you without having to bake the product in the bread machine. This is great if you want to make things like pizzas, which need really elastic dough – which is often slow and frustrating to mix by hand.

Simply set your bread machine to the right setting, make sure you know when it will finish, and then be around to take the dough out. If you want to make pizzas, you can then shape them on your counter and bake them in the oven. Do this for any kinds of dough that you wish to mix.

Chapter 1: Fruit Bread Recipes

Strawberry Bread

Preparation Time: 10 minutes
Cooking Time: 4 hours
Servings: 10 slices

Ingredients:
- 5 eggs, pasteurized
- 1 egg white, pasteurized
- 5 g (1½ tsp) vanilla extract
- 30 g (2 tbsp) heavy whipping cream
- 30 g (2 tbsp) sour cream
- 140g (5 oz/1 cup) monk fruit powder
- 20 g (1½ tsp) baking powder
- 5 g (½ tsp) salt
- 5 g (½ tsp) cinnamon
- 115 g (4 oz/8 tbsp) butter, melted
- 110 g (4 oz/¾ cup) flour
- 120 g (¾ cup) strawberries, chopped

Directions:
1. Take a large bowl, crack eggs and then beat in egg white, vanilla, heavy cream, sour cream, baking powder, salt, and cinnamon until well combined.
2. Then stir in flour and fold in strawberries until mixed.
3. Add batter into the bread bucket, shut the lid, select the BASIC/WHITE cycle or LOW-CARBS setting and then press the UP/DOWN arrow button to adjust baking time according to the bread machine; it will take 3–4 hours.
4. Then press the crust button to select light crust if available, and press the START/STOP button to switch on the bread machine.
5. When the bread machine beeps, open the lid, take out the bread basket, and lift the bread.
6. Let bread cool on a wire rack for one hour, then cut it into ten slices and serve.

Nutritional Content
Calories: 200.2; Fat: 14.4 g; Carbs: 4.1 g; Protein: 5.7 g

Lemon Bread

Preparation Time: 15 minutes
Cooking Time: 1 hour
Servings: 12 slices

Ingredients:
- 105 g (9.5 oz/ ¾ cup) flour
- 5 g (½ tsp) baking powder
- 100 g (3.5 oz/½ cup) sugar
- 20 g (3.5 oz/2 tbsp) poppy seeds
- Zest from 2 lemons
- 30 ml (2 tbsp) lemon juice
- 40 g (1.5 oz/3 tbsp) butter, melted
- 6 whole eggs

For the Icing:
- 100 g (4 oz/½ cup) sugar
- 15 ml (1 tbsp) lemon juice
- 30 ml (2 tbsp) water

Directions:
1. Put all ingredients into the bread machine pan. Close the lid.
2. Set the bread machine program to CAKE. The time may vary depending on the device.
3. Press START. Help the machine to knead the dough, if necessary.
4. After 40 minutes of baking, start checking for doneness using a toothpick. The approximate baking time is 45–55 minutes.
5. Wait until the program is complete, and when done, take the bucket out and let it cool for 10 minutes.
6. Shake the loaf from the pan and let it cool for 30 minutes on a cooling rack.
7. Make the icing in a small bowl, mixing all the ingredients. Drizzle it over the bread.
8. Slice and serve.

Nutritional Content
Calories: 191.2; Carbs: 14.9 g; Fat: 15.7 g

Marzipan Cherry Bread

Preparation Time: 3 hours
Cooking Time: 35 minutes
Servings: 8

Ingredients:
- 1 egg
- 180 ml (6 oz/¾ cup) milk
- 15 ml (0.5 oz/1 tbsp) almond liqueur
- 60 ml (2 oz/4 tbsp) orange juice
- 55 g (2 oz/½ cup) ground almonds
- 60 g (2 oz/¼ cup) butter
- 70 g (2 oz/1/3 cup) sugar
- 380 g (14 oz/4 cups) almond flour
- 10 g (1 tbsp) instant yeast
- 5 g (1 tsp) salt
- 120 g (4 oz/½ cup) marzipan
- 85 g (3 oz/½ cup) dried cherries, pitted

Directions:
1. Put all ingredients into the bread machine, carefully following the instructions of the manufacturer (except marzipan and cherry).
2. Set the program of the bread machine to basic/sweet and set the crust type to light or medium.
3. Press START.
4. Once the machine beeps, add marzipan and cherry. When the cycle is completed, take the bucket out and let the loaf cool for 5 minutes.
5. Shake the bucket gently to remove the loaf, then transfer to a cooling rack, slice, and serve.

Nutritional Content
Calories 508.1; Carbs 3.1 g; Fat: 14.4 g; Protein 18.2 g

Lemon Raspberry Loaf

Preparation Time: 10 minutes
Cooking Time: 4 hours
Servings: 2 pounds / 12 slices

Ingredients:
- 2 eggs, pasteurized
- 60 g (2 oz/4 tbsp) sour cream
- 5 ml (1 tsp) vanilla extract, unsweetened
- 5 ml (1 tsp) lemon extract, unsweetened
- 60 g (2 oz/4 tbsp) unsalted butter, melted
- 100 g (3.5 oz/¼ cup) sugar
- 30 ml (2 tbsp) lemon juice
- 60 g (2 oz/½ cup) raspberries preserve
- 280 g (10 oz/2 cups) flour
- 15 g (1½ tsp) baking powder

Directions:
1. Take a large bowl, place flour in it, and then stir in baking soda until mixed.
2. Take a separate large bowl, crack eggs in it, beat in sour cream, extracts, butter, sugar, and lemon juice until blended, and then stir in raspberry preserve until just combined.
3. Add egg mixture into the bread bucket, top with flour mixture, shut the lid, select the BASIC/WHITE cycle setting and then press the UP/DOWN arrow button to adjust baking time according to the bread machine; it will take 3–4 hours.
4. Then press the crust button to select light crust if available, and press the START/STOP button to switch on the bread machine. When the bread machine beeps, open the lid, take out the bread basket, and lift the bread.
5. Let bread cool on a wire rack for one hour, then cut it into twelve slices and serve.

Nutritional Content
Calories: 168.2; Fat: 12.3 g; Carbs: 4.5 g; Fiber: 2.1 g; Protein: 5.6 g

Blueberry Bread

Preparation Time: 10 minutes
Cooking Time: 50 minutes
Servings: 12 slices

Ingredients:
- 75 g (2.6 oz/ ½ cup) blueberries
- 70 g (2.7 oz/ 1/3 cup) sugar
- 5 g (2 tsp) baking powder
- 285 g (10 oz/2 cups) flour
- 60 g (4 tbsp) sour cream
- 60 g (2 oz/4 tbsp) unsalted butter, melted
- 2 whole eggs
- 5 g (1 tsp) vanilla

Directions:
1. In a large bowl, beat eggs with an electric mixer well.
2. Pour them into the bread machine pan. Add all other ingredients. Close the lid.
3. Set the bread machine program to CAKE for 45–60 minutes (depending on the device).
4. Press START. After the signal indicating the beginning of the BAKE mode, add the blueberries.
5. After 35 minutes of baking, start checking for doneness using a toothpick. The approximate baking time is 45–50 minutes. Wait until the program is complete. When done, take the bucket out and let it cool for 10 minutes.
6. Shake the loaf from the pan and let it cool for 30 minutes on a cooling rack.
7. Slice and serve.

Nutritional Content
Calories: 163.5; Carbs: 10.2 g; Fat: 11.5 g

Apple Chunk Bread

Preparation Time: 15 minutes
Cooking Time: 1 hour and 30 minutes
Servings: 8

Ingredients:
- 425 g (15 oz/3 cups) bread flour, unbleached
- 1 g (½ teaspoon) ground cinnamon
- 2 apples, peeled and diced
- 25 g (0.1 oz/2 tablespoons) sugar
- 20 g (0.8 oz/2 ½ teaspoons) yeast
- 60 ml (2 oz/¼ cup) olive oil
- 10 g (0.3 oz/1½ teaspoons) salt
- 240 ml (1 cup) milk, at room temperature

Directions:
1. Add ingredients except apple to a bread machine according to the manufacturer's instructions and pour in milk and oil in its pan.
2. Add sugar, cinnamon, salt, and flour, and then insert the pan into the bread machine.
3. Plug in the bread machine, press the setting for "knead," and press the "start" button.
4. When done, add the apples, press the setting for "sweet quick bread," set the crust color to "light" or "medium," and then press start and let it bake.
5. When the bread cycle is done, take out the pan and then let the bread loaf rest in the pan for 10 minutes.
6. Then transfer the bread loaf to a wire rack and let it cool completely.
7. When ready to eat, cut the bread loaf into slices and then serve.

Nutritional Content
Calories: 321; Carbs: 32.2 g; Fat: 9.5 g, Protein: 6.3 g

Banana Bread

Preparation Time: 10 minutes
Cooking Time: 60–70 minutes
Servings: 16 slices

Ingredients:
- 355 g (12.5 oz/2½) cup flour
- 2 large bananas, mashed
- 6 large eggs, beaten
- 20 g (4 tbsp) ghee, melted
- 200 g (7 oz/½ cup) sugar
- 30 g (2 tbsp) cinnamon
- 15 g (1 tbsp) baking powder
- 15 g (0.5 oz/½ cup) walnuts, crushed
- 5 g (1 tsp) ground nutmeg

Directions:
1. In a large bowl, combine all of the dry ingredients. In a small bowl, beat the eggs with an electric mixer.
2. Pour eggs and all of the wet ingredients into the bread machine pan.
3. Cover them with dry ingredients. Close the lid.
4. Set the bread machine program to DOUGH. The time may vary depending on the device. Press START.
5. After the program completes, start the Bake mode for 55 minutes. After 45 minutes of baking, start checking for doneness using a toothpick. The approximate baking time is 45–60 minutes. Wait until the program is complete. When done, take the bucket out and let it cool for 10 minutes. Shake the loaf from the pan and let it cool for 30 minutes on a cooling rack.
6. Slice and serve.

Nutritional Content
Calories: 187.1; Carbs: 8.9 g; Fat 12.2 g

Sweet Avocado Bread

Preparation Time: 10 minutes
Cooking Time: 4 hours
Servings: 6

Ingredients:
- 3 eggs, pasteurized
- 10 g (0.5 oz/2 tbsp) sugar
- 10 g (1 tbsp) vanilla extract
- 2 ripe medium avocados, mashed
- 55 g (1.9 oz/6 tbsp) flour
- 5 g (¾ tsp. baking soda
- 5 g (½ tsp) salt
- 15 g (2 tbsp) cocoa powder, unsweetened

Directions:
1. Take a large bowl, crack eggs, beat in sweetener and vanilla until fluffy, and then mix in avocado.
2. Take a separate large bowl, place flour, and then stir in the remaining ingredients until mixed.
3. Add egg mixture into the bread bucket, top with flour mixture, shut the lid, select the BASIC/WHITE cycle or LOW-CARBS setting, and then press the UP/DOWN arrow button to adjust baking time according to the bread machine; it will take 3–4 hours. Then press the crust button to select light crust if available, and press the START/STOP button to switch on the bread machine.
4. When the bread machine beeps, open the lid, take out the bread basket, and lift the bread.
5. Let bread cool on a wire rack for 1 hour, then cut it into twelve slices and serve.

Nutritional Content
Calories 91.3; Fat: 4.1 g; Carbs: 2.2 g; Fiber: 2.5 g; Protein: 8.2 g

Cranberry and Orange Bread

Preparation Time: 10 minutes
Cooking Time: 4 hours
Servings: 6

Ingredients:
- 100 g (1 cup) cranberries, chopped
- 2/3 cup+3 tbsp. monk fruit powder, divided
- 5 eggs, pasteurized
- 1 egg white, pasteurized
- 30 g (2 tbsp) sour cream
- 1½ tsp. orange extract
- 5 g (1 tsp) vanilla extract
- 130 g (5 oz/9 tbsp) unsalted butter, melted
- 80 g (3 oz/9 tbsp) flour
- 5 g (1 ½ tsp) baking powder
- 5 g (¼ tsp) salt

Directions:
1. Take a small bowl, place cranberries, and then stir in 4 tbsp. of monk fruit powder until combined. Set aside until required.
2. Take a large bowl, crack eggs in it, beat in remaining ingredients in it in the order described in the ingredients until incorporated, and then fold in cranberries until just mixed.
3. Add batter into the bread bucket, shut the lid, select the BASIC/WHITE cycle or LOW-CARBS setting and then press the UP/DOWN arrow button to adjust baking time according to the bread machine; it will take 3–4 hours.
4. Then press the crust button to select light crust if available, and press the START/STOP button to switch on the bread machine.
5. When the bread machine beeps, open the lid, take out the bread basket, and lift the bread.
6. Let bread cool on a wire rack for one hour, then cut it into twelve slices and serve.

Nutritional Content
Calories: 141.3; Fat: 12.1 g; Carbs: 2.4 g; Fiber: 1.2 g; Protein: 5.9 g

Citrus Bread

Preparation Time: 3 hours
Cooking Time: 1 hour
Servings: 8

Ingredients:
- 1 egg
- 40 g (3 tbsp) butter
- 70 g (2 oz/ 1/3) cup sugar
- 5 g (1 tbsp) vanilla sugar
- 120 ml (½ cup orange juice)
- 160 ml (2/3 cup) milk
- 5 g (1 tsp) salt
- 450 g (15 oz/4 cups) almond flour
- 10 g (1 tbsp) instant yeast
- 55 g (2 oz/¼ cup) oranges, candied
- 55 g (2 oz/¼ cup) lemon, candied
- 2 tsp. lemon zest
- 25 g (1 oz/¼ cup) almonds, chopped

Directions:
1. Put all ingredients into the bread machine, carefully following the instructions of the manufacturer (except candied fruits, zest, and almonds).
2. Set the program of the bread machine to basic/sweet and set the crust type to light or medium.
3. Press START. Once the machine beeps, add candied fruits, lemon zest, and chopped almonds.
4. When the cycle is completed, take the bucket out and let the loaf cool for 5 minutes.
5. Shake the bucket gently to remove the loaf, then transfer to a cooling rack, slice, and serve.

Nutritional Content
Calories 402.4; Carbs 3.4 g; Fat 7.1 g; Protein 12.8 g

Apricot Prune Bread

Preparation Time: 3 hours
Cooking Time: 20 minutes
Servings: 8

Ingredients:
- 1 egg
- 180 ml (¾ cup) whole milk
- 50 ml (¼ cup) apricot juice
- 55 g (2 oz/¼ cup) butter
- 40 g (1.5 oz/ 1/5 cup) sugar
- 570 g (20 oz/4 cups) flour
- 10 g (1 tbsp) instant yeast
- 5 g (¼ tsp) salt
- 60 g (2 oz/¾ cup) prunes, chopped
- 50 g (1.7 oz/¾ cup) dried apricots, chopped

Directions:
1. Put all ingredients into the bread machine, carefully following the manufacturer's instructions (except apricots and prunes).
2. Set the program of the bread machine to basic/sweet and set the crust type to light or medium.
3. Press START. Once the machine beeps, add apricots and prunes.
4. When the cycle is completed, take the bucket out and let the loaf cool for 5 minutes.
5. Shake the bucket gently to remove the loaf, then transfer to a cooling rack, slice, and serve.

Nutritional Content
Calories 362.5; Carbs 2.4 g; Fat 6.2 g; Protein 11.9 g

Raisin Bread

Preparation Time: 2 hours
Cooking time: 1 hour
Servings: 4

Ingredients:
- 1 egg
- 1 cup (8 oz) milk
- ¼ cup (2 oz) butter
- ¼ cup (1.78 oz) sugar
- 4 cups (18 oz) all-purpose flour/bread flour
- 10 g (1 tablespoon) instant yeast
- 5 g (1 teaspoon) salt
- 170 g (6 oz/½ cup) raisins

Directions:
1. Follow the manufacturer's instructions carefully and put all the ingredients into the bread machine (except raisins). Set the program of the bread machine to BASIC/SWEET and set the crust type to LIGHT or MEDIUM. Press START. Once the machine beeps, add raisins. When the cycle is completed, take the bucket out and let the loaf cool for 5 minutes.
2. Shake the bucket gently to remove the loaf, then transfer to a cooling rack, slice, and serve.

Nutritional Content
Calories 367.8; Fat 5.7 g; Carbs 65.6 g; Protein 11.2 g

Raisin Candied Fruit Bread

Preparation Time: 10 minutes
Cooking Time: 3 hours
Servings: 8

Ingredients:
- 1 egg, beaten
- 295 ml (1¼ cup) lukewarm water
- 2g (½ tsp) ground cardamom
- 5 g (½ tsp) table salt
- 19 g (1½ tbsp) sugar
- 55g (1.9oz/¼ cup) butter, melted
- 410 g (14.4 oz/3 cups) bread flour
- 3 g (1 tsp) bread machine yeast
- 50 g (1.7oz/ 1/3 cup) raisins
- 225 g (7.9 oz/ 1/3 cup) mixed candied fruit

Directions:
1. Add all of the ingredients except for the candied fruits and raisins to the bread pan according to the manufacturer's instructions.
2. Place the pan in the bread machine and close the lid.
3. Turn on the bread maker. Select thc White/Basic or Fruit/Nut setting, then the loaf size, and finally the crust color. Start the cycle.
4. When the machine signals to add ingredients, add the candied fruits and raisins.
5. When the cycle is finished and the bread is baked, carefully remove the pan from the machine. Use a potholder as the handle will be very hot. Let it rest for a few minutes.
6. Remove the bread from the pan and allow it to cool on a wire rack for at least 10 minutes before slicing.

Nutritional Content
Calories: 206; Fat: 4.6 g; Carbs: 33.4 g; Protein: 4.7 g

Spice Peach Bread

Preparation Time: 10 minutes
Cooking Time: 3 hours
Servings: 7

Ingredients:

- 80 g (2.8 oz/ 1/3 cup) lukewarm heavy whipping cream
- 1 egg, beaten
- 15 g (1 tbsp) unsalted butter, melted
- 15 g (2¼ tbsps.) sugar
- ½ teaspoons table salt
- 2 g (1 tsp) nutmeg, ground
- 1 g (1/3 tsp) cinnamon, ground
- 340 g (11.9 oz/ 2 2/3 cups) white bread flour
- 40 g (1.4 oz/ 1/3 cup) whole-wheat flour
- 5 g (1⅛ tsp) bread machine yeast
- 185 g (6.5 oz/ ¾ cup) canned peaches, drained and chopped

Directions:

1. Add all of the ingredients except for the peach to the bread pan according to the manufacturer's instructions.
2. Place the pan in the bread machine and close the lid.
3. Turn on the bread maker. Select the White/Basic or Fruit/Nut setting, then the loaf size, and finally the crust color. Start the machine.
4. When the machine signals to add ingredients, add the peaches.
5. When the cycle is finished and the bread is baked, carefully remove the pan from the machine. Let it rest for a few minutes.
6. Remove the bread from the pan and allow it to cool on a wire rack for at least 10 minutes before slicing.

Nutritional Content
Calories: 157; Fat: 3.1 g; Carbs: 26.4 g; Protein: 4.2 g

Strawberry Oat Bread

Preparation Time: 5 minutes
Cooking Time: 3 hours
Servings: 8

Ingredients:
- 265 ml (1⅛ cups) lukewarm milk
- 45 g (1.6 oz/3 tbsps.) unsalted butter, melted
- 40 g (1.4 oz/3 tbsps.) sugar
- 5 g (½ tsp) salt
- 80 g (2.8 oz/1 cup) quick oats
- 390 g (13.8 oz/2¼ cups) bread flour
- 5g (1½ tsp) bread machine yeast
- 150 g (5.3 oz/¾ cup) strawberries, sliced

Directions:
1. Add all of the ingredients except for the strawberries to the bread pan according to the manufacturer's instructions.
2. Place the pan in the bread machine and close the lid.
3. Turn on the bread maker. Select the White/Basic or Fruit/Nut setting, then the loaf size, and finally the crust color. Start the cycle.
4. When the machine signals to add ingredients, add the strawberries.
5. When the cycle is finished and the bread is baked, carefully remove the pan from the machine. Use a potholder as the handle will be very hot. Let it rest for a few minutes.
6. Remove the bread from the pan and allow it to cool on a wire rack for at least 10 minutes before slicing.

Nutritional Content
Calories: 164; Fat: 3.8 g; Carbs: 26.7 g; Protein: 4 g.

Cocoa Date Bread

Preparation Time: 10 minutes
Cooking Time: 2 hours 10 minutes
Servings: 8

Ingredients:

- 180 ml (¾ cup) lukewarm water
- 30 g (1 oz/2 tbsps.) unsalted butter, melted
- 85g (3 oz/¼ cup) honey
- 12 g (1 tbsp) sugar
- 5 g (1 tsp) table salt
- 165 g (5.8 oz/2¼ cups) whole-wheat flour
- 5 g (1 tbsp) cocoa powder, unsweetened
- 5 g (1½ tsp) bread machine yeast
- 170 g (6 oz/¾ cup) chopped dates

Directions:

1. Add all of the ingredients except for the dates to the bread pan according to the manufacturer's instructions.
2. Place the pan in the bread machine and close the lid.
3. Turn on the bread maker. Select the White/Basic or Fruit/Nut setting, then the loaf size, and finally the crust color. Start the cycle.
4. When the machine signals to add ingredients, add the dates.
5. When the cycle is finished and the bread is baked, carefully remove the pan from the machine. Use a potholder as the handle will be very hot. Let it rest for a few minutes.
6. Remove the bread from the pan and allow it to cool on a wire rack for at least 10 minutes before slicing.

Nutritional Content
Calories: 221; Fat: 2.7 g; Carbs: 38.6 g; Protein: 4.8 g

Fruit Syrup Bread

Preparation Time: 10 minutes
Cooking Time: 25 minutes
Servings: 8

Ingredients:

- 460 g (16 oz/ 3 2/3 cups whole wheat flour
- 5 g (1 ½ tsp) instant yeast
- 60 g (2.1 oz/¼ cup) unsalted butter, melted
- 240 ml (1 cup) lukewarm water
- 25 g (2 tbsps.) sugar
- 25 g (¼ cup) rolled oats
- 5 g (½ tsp) salt
- 125 ml (½ cup) syrup from preserved fruit

Directions:

1. Preparing the Ingredients. Combine the syrup and 1/2 cup water. Heat until lukewarm. Add more water to precisely 1 cup of water.
2. Place all the ingredients, except for the rolled oats and butter, in a liquid-dry-yeast layering.
3. Put the pan in the bread machine.
4. Load the rolled oats in the automatic dispenser.
5. Select the Bake cycle. Choose whole-wheat loaf.
6. Press start and wait until the loaf is cooked.
7. Brush the top with butter once cooked.
8. The machine will start the keep warm mode after the bread is complete.
9. Let it remain in that mode for about 10 minutes before unplugging.
10. Remove the pan and let it cool down for about 10 minutes.

Nutritional Content
Calories 277; Carbs: 48.4 g; Fat 3 g; Protein 9.4 g

Chapter 2: Vegetable and Fruit Bread Recipes

Cauliflower and Garlic Bread

Preparation Time: 10 minutes
Cooking Time: 4 hours
Servings: 9

Ingredients:
- 5 eggs, separated
- 75 g (2.6 oz/ 2/3 cup) coconut flour
- 160 g (5.6 oz/1½ cup rice cauliflower
- 5 g (1 tsp) garlic, minced
- 5 g (½ tsp) sea salt
- 5 g (½ tbsp) rosemary, chopped
- 5 g (½ tbsp) parsley, chopped
- 10 g (¾ tbsp) baking powder
- 45 g (1.5 oz/3 tbsp) unsalted butter

Directions:
1. Place the cauliflower rice in a bowl and cover it. Microwave for 3–4 minutes or until steaming. Then drain. Wrap in cheesecloth and remove as much moisture as possible. Set aside.
2. Place egg whites in a bowl and whisk until stiff peaks form.
3. Then transfer ¼ of the whipped egg whites into a food for. Add remaining ingredients except for cauliflower and pulse for 2 minutes until blended.
4. Add cauliflower rice, and pulse for 2 minutes until combined. Then pulse in the remaining egg whites until just mixed.
5. Add batter into the bread bucket and cover. Select the BASIC/WHITE cycle. Press START.
6. Remove the bread when done. Cool, slice, and serve.

Nutritional Content
Calories: 105.8; Fat: 6.8 g; Carbs: 2.3 g; Protein: 9.6 g

Zucchini Bread

Preparation Time: 1 hour
Cooking Time: 1 hour 10 minutes
Servings: 4

Ingredients:

- 2 eggs
- 1 g (¼ tsp. salt)
- 200 ml (1 cup) oil
- 200 g (7 oz/ 1 cup) white sugar
- 5 g (1 tbsp) vanilla sugar
- 5 g (2 tsps.) cinnamon
- 100 g (½ cup) nuts, ground
- 350 g (12.3 oz/3 cups) all-purpose flour, well sifted
- 5 g (1 tbsp) baking powder
- 130 g (4.5 oz/1¼ cups) zucchini, grated

Directions:

1. Add all of the ingredients to your bread machine (except the zucchini), carefully following the instructions of the manufacturer.
2. Set the program of your bread machine to CAKE/SWEET and set the crust type to LIGHT.
3. Press START.
4. Once the machine beeps, add zucchini.
5. Wait until the cycle completes.
6. Once the loaf is ready, take the bucket out and let the loaf cool for 5 minutes.
7. Gently shake the bucket to remove the loaf.
8. Transfer to a cooling rack, slice, and serve.

Nutritional Content
Calories 556, Fat 31 g, Carbs: 64.3 g, Fiber 3.1 g, Protein 8.6 g

Pumpkin and Sunflower Seed Bread

Preparation time: 40 minutes
Cooking time: 40 minutes
Servings: 10

Ingredients:

- 75 g (2.6 oz./½ cup) psyllium husk, ground
- 85 g (3 oz/½ cup) chia seeds
- 30 g (1.1 oz/½ cup) pumpkin seeds
- 70 g (2.3 oz/½ cup) sunflower seeds
- 20 g (2 tbsp) flaxseed, ground
- 5 g (1 tsp) baking soda
- 1 g (¼ tsp) salt
- 45 ml (3 tbsp) oil
- 1¼ cup egg whites
- 120 ml (½ cup) milk

Directions:

1. Place all wet ingredients into the bread machine pan first.
2. Add dry ingredients. Set the bread machine to the gluten-free setting.
3. When it is done, remove the bread machine pan from the bread machine.
4. Let cool slightly before transferring to a cooling rack.
5. You can store the bread for up to 5 days in the refrigerator.

Nutritional Content
Calories 150.5; Carbs 12.4 g; Fat 7.8 g; Protein 6.5

Carrot Bread

Preparation Time: 1 hour
Cooking Time: 1 hour 10 minutes
Servings: 4

Ingredients:
- 4 eggs
- 1 g (¼ tsp) kosher salt
- 100 g (½ cup / 4 oz.) butter
- 120 g (½ cup / 4 oz.) sugar
- 10 g (1 Tbsp) vanilla sugar
- 5 g (2 tsp.) cinnamon
- 350 g (13.5 oz /3 cups) all-purpose flour
- 15 g (1 tbsp) baking powder
- 50 g (1.7 oz/¼ cup) ground nuts
- 150 g (5.3 oz/¾ cup) carrot, grated

Directions:
1. Add all of the ingredients to your bread machine (except the carrot), carefully following the instructions of the manufacturer.
2. Set the program of your bread machine to CAKE/SWEET and set the crust type to LIGHT.
3. Press START.
4. Once the machine beeps, add a grated carrot.
5. Wait until the cycle completes.
6. Once the loaf is ready, take the bucket out and let the loaf cool for 5 minutes.
7. Gently shake the bucket to remove the loaf.
8. Transfer to a cooling rack, slice, and serve.

Nutritional Content
Calories 398, Fat 17.3 g, Carbs: 53 g, Protein 9.2 g

Almond Pumpkin Bread

Preparation Time: 10 minutes
Cooking Time: 60 minutes
Servings: 16

Ingredients:
- 80 ml (1/3 cup) oil
- 3 large eggs
- 340 g (12 oz/1 ½ cups) pumpkin puree
- 200 g (7.1 oz/1 cup) granulated sugar
- 10 g (1½ tsp) baking powder
- 5 g (½ tsp) baking soda
- 1 g (¼ tsp) salt
- 2 g (¾ tsp) cinnamon, ground
- 1 g (¼ tsp) nutmeg, ground
- 1 g (½ tsp) ginger, ground
- 290 g (10.1 oz/3 cups) almond flour
- 55 g (2 oz/½ cup) pecans, chopped

Directions:
1. Grease the bread machine pan with cooking spray. Stir all the wet ingredients in a bowl. Add all the dry ingredients except pecans until mixed.
2. Pour the batter onto the bread machine pan and place it back inside the bread machine. Close and select QUICK BREAD. Add the pecans after the beep. Remove the bread when done. Cool, slice, and serve.

Nutritional Content
Calories: 52.4; Fat: 12.3 g; Carbs: 5.3 g; Protein: 11.6 g

Beetroot Bread

Preparation Time: 30 minutes
Cooking Time: 45 minutes
Servings: 2

Ingredients:

- 150 g (5.3 oz/1 cup) fresh beetroot, grated
- 100 g (3.3 oz/1 cup) almond flour
- 55 g (2 oz/½ cup) coconut flour
- 1 g (½ tsp) nutmeg, ground
- 1 g (¼ tsp) cinnamon, ground
- 10 g (2 tsp). active dry yeast
- 65 g (1/3 cup) Swerve sweetener
- 120 ml (4 oz/½ cup) warm water
- 60 g (2 oz4 tsp) unsalted butter, melted
- 35 g (1.2 oz/ 1/3 cup) walnuts, roasted and sliced
- 5 g (1 tsp). baking powder
- 5 g (¼ tsp) salt

Directions:

1. Get a mixing container and combine the almond flour, coconut flour, roasted walnuts, Swerve sweetener, cinnamon ground, nutmeg powder, and baking powder.
2. Get another container and combine the warm water, shredded beetroot, and melted unsalted butter.
3. As per the instructions in the machine manual, pour the ingredients in the bread pan, taking care to follow how to mix in the yeast.
4. In the machine, place the bread pan, select the sweet bread setting - together with the crust type if available - then press start once you have closed the lid of the machine.
5. When the bread is ready, remove the bread pan from the machine. Use a stainless spatula to extract the bread from the pan and turn the pan upside down on a metallic rack where the bread will cool off before slicing it.

Nutritional Content
Calories 852.4; Fat 41.4 g; Carbs 100.3 g; Protein 23.4 g

Tomato Bread

Preparation Time: 15 minutes
Cooking Time: 45 minutes
Servings: 3

Ingredients:

- 4 whole eggs
- 30 g (1 oz/2 tbsp) salted butter, melted
- 135 g (4.5 oz/1 cup) flaxseed meal
- 10 g (4 tsp) oat fiber
- 10 g (2 tsp) baking powder
- 10 ml (1½ tsp) xanthan gum
- 5 g (¼ tsp) sea salt
- 5 g (½ tsp) basil, dried
- 1 g (¼ tsp) garlic powder
- 10 g (2 tbsp) sun-dried tomatoes, diced
- 25 g (1 oz/¼ cup) parmesan, grated

Directions:

1. Carefully whisk eggs and butter together. Pour all the ingredients into the bread machine pan.
2. Close the lid. Set the bread machine program to CAKE for 30–45 minutes (depending on the bread machine model) and choose the crust color LIGHT. Press START. Help the bread machine knead the dough with a spatula, if necessary. Before the baking mode begins, sprinkle the top with grated parmesan.
3. After baking for 20 minutes, check for doneness with a toothpick. Wait until the program is complete, then take the bucket out and let it cool for 5–10 minutes.
4. Shake the loaf from the pan and let it cool for 30 minutes on a cooling rack.
5. Slice and serve.

Nutritional Content
Calories 87.8; Carbs 2.2 g; Fat 5.1 g; Protein 12.2 g

Orange Bread

Preparation Time: 10 minutes
Cooking Time: 2-4 hours
Servings: 12

Ingredients:

- 235 ml milk, at 25°C(80°F)
- 45 g (1.5 oz) freshly squeezed orange juice, at room temperature
- 45 g (1.5 oz) sugar
- 5 g instant yeast
- 15 g (0.5 oz) melted butter, cooled
- 5 g (1 tsp) salt
- 705 g (24.9 oz) white bread flour
- Zest of 1 orange

Directions:

1. Add the ingredients to your bread machine as suggested by the manufacturer.
2. Select Basic/White bread and medium or light crust, and select Start button.
3. Once the loaf is done, remove the bucket from the machine.
4. Let the loaf cool for 5 minutes.
5. Remove the loaf and put on a rack to cool.

Nutritional Content

Calories: 147; Protein: 4 g; Fat: 2 g; Carbs: 28 g

Onion Bread

Preparation time: 20 minutes
Cooking time: 5 minutes
Servings: 6

Ingredients:

- 1 red onion, diced and sautéed with ½ tsp. butter until golden brown
- 15 g (0.5 oz/3 tsps.) unsalted butter, melted
- 5 g (¼ tsp) salt
- 1 g (¼ tsp) garlic, ground
- 1 g (3 tsp) psyllium husk flour
- 5 eggs
- 2 g (½ tsp) baking powder
- 2 g (¾ tsp) active dry yeast
- 1 g ½ tsp. onion powder
- 100 g (3.5 oz/1 cup) almond flour

Directions:

1. Get a mixing container and combine the almond flour, salt, psyllium husk flour, ground onion, baking powder, and ground garlic.
2. Get another mixing container and mix the melted unsalted butter, eggs, and sautéed onions.
3. As per the instructions on the manual of your machine, pour the ingredients in the bread pan, also following the instructions for the yeast.
4. Place the bread pan in the machine, and select the basic bread setting, together with the bread size and crust type, if available, then press start once you have closed the lid of the machine.
5. When the bread is ready, extract it, and place it on a metallic mesh surface to cool completely before cutting and eating it.

Nutritional Content
Calories: 127; Fat: 9.48 g; Carbs: 2.07 g; Protein: 7.97 g.

Date Bread

Preparation Time: 10 minutes
Cooking Time: 2-4 hours
Servings: 12

Ingredients:
- 175 ml (¾ cup) water, at 25°C (80°F)
- 120 ml milk, at 25°C (80°F)
- 30 g (1 oz) melted butter, cooled
- 60 ml (¼ cup) honey
- 45 g (1.5 oz) molasses
- 15 g (0.5 oz) sugar
- 30 g (1 oz) skim milk powder
- 5 g (½ tsp) salt
- 530 g (18.7 oz) whole-wheat flour
- 290g (10.2 oz) white bread flour
- 15 g (0.5 oz) unsweetened cocoa powder
- 5 g instant yeast
- 175 g (6.1 oz) chopped dates

Directions:
1. Place the ingredients, except the dates, in your bread machine as suggested by the manufacturer.
2. Select Basic/White bread and medium or light crust, and select Start button.
3. When the machine signals, add the chopped dates, or put them in the nut/raisin hopper and automatically add them.
4. When ready, remove bucket from the bread machine.
5. Let the loaf stand for 5 minutes.
6. Remove the loaf from bucket and put on a rack to cool.

Nutritional Content
Calories: 233; Protein: 5 g; Fat: 3 g; Carbs: 42 g

Zucchini Herbed Bread

Preparation Time: 2 hours 20 minutes
Cooking Time: 50 minutes
Servings: 1 loaf

Ingredients:
- 235 ml (½ cup) water
- 10 g (2 tsp) honey
- 15 ml (1 tbsp) oil
- 80 g (2.8 oz/¾ cup) zucchini, grated
- 100 g (3.5 oz/¾ cup) whole wheat flour
- 240 g (8.5 oz/2 cups) bread flour
- 1 g (1 tbsp) fresh basil, chopped
- 5 g (2 tsp) sesame seeds
- 5 g (1 tsp) salt
- 5 g (1½ tsp) active dry yeast

Directions:
1. Add all of the ingredients to your bread machine, carefully following the instructions of the manufacturer
2. Set the program of your bread machine to Basic/White Bread and set crust type to Medium
3. Press START
4. Wait until the cycle completes
5. Once the loaf is ready, take the bucket out and let the loaf cool for 5 minutes
6. Gently shake the bucket to remove the loaf
7. Transfer to a cooling rack, slice and serve

Nutritional Content
Calories: 153; Fat: 1 g; Carbs: 28 g; Protein: 5 g

Plum Orange Bread

Preparation Time: 10 minutes
Cooking Time: 2-4 hours
Servings: 12

Ingredients:
- 265 ml (1 1/3 cup) water, at 25°C (80°F)
- 35 g (1.2 oz) melted butter, cooled
- 45 g (1.5 oz) sugar
- 5 g (1 tsp) salt
- 5 g (1 tsp) orange zest
- 1 g (½ tsp) ground cinnamon
- 1 g (a pinch) ground nutmeg
- 440 g (15.5oz) whole-wheat flour
- 265 g (1.5 oz) white bread flour
- 10 g (2 tbsp) instant yeast
- 235 g (8.2 oz) chopped fresh plums

Directions:
1. Place the ingredients, except the plums, in your bread machine as per your manufacture's suggestions.
2. Select Basic/White bread, select medium or light crust, and press Start.
3. Once the machine signals, add the chopped plums.
4. Once the loaf is done, remove the bucket from the machine.
5. Let the loaf cool for five minutes.
6. Remove the loaf from bucket and put on a rack to cool.

Nutritional Content
Calories: 141; Protein: 3 g; Fat: 3 g; Carbs: 26 g

Keto Spinach Bread

Preparation time: 10 minutes
Cooking time: 30 minutes
Servings: 10

Ingredients:

- 15 g (½ cup) spinach, chopped
- 15 ml (1 tbsp) olive oil
- 235 ml (1 cup) water
- 390 g (13.8/3 cups) almond flour
- 1 g (a pinch) of salt and black pepper
- 1 g (1 tbsp) stevia
- 5 g (1 tsp) baking powder
- 5 g (1 tsp) baking soda
- 120 g (4.2 oz/½ cup) cheddar, shredded

Directions:

1. Add all of the ingredients to your bread machine, carefully following the instructions of the manufacturer.
2. Set the program of your bread machine to Basic and set the crust type to light. Press START.
3. When ready, cool the bread down, slice, and serve.

Nutritional Content

Calories: 142; Fat: 7 g; Carbs: 5 g; Protein: 6 g

Blueberry Oatmeal Bread

Preparation Time: 10 minutes
Cooking Time: 2-4 hours
Servings: 12

Ingredients:

- 175 ml (¾ cup) milk, at 25°C (80°F)
- 1 egg
- 35 g (1.2 oz) melted butter, cooled
- 25 ml (1/8 cup) honey
- 120 g (4.2 oz) rolled oats
- 550 g (19.4 oz) white bread flour
- 5g (½ tsp) salt
- 10 g (2 tbsps.) instant yeast
- 120 g (4.2 oz) dried blueberries

Directions:

1. Place the ingredients, except the blueberries, in your bread machine as recommended by the manufacturer.
2. Select Basic/White bread and medium or light crust, and select Start button.
3. Add the blueberries when the machine signals or 5 minutes before the second kneading cycle is finished.
4. Once the loaf is done, remove the bucket from the machine.
5. Let the loaf cool for five minutes.
6. Remove the loaf from bucket and put on a rack to cool.

Nutritional Content
Calories: 147; Protein: 4 g; Fat: 3 g; Carbs: 25 g

Red Bell Pepper Bread

Preparation time: 10 minutes
Cooking time: 30 minutes
Servings: 12

Ingredients:

- 140 g (1½ cups) red bell peppers, chopped
- 5 g (1 tsp) baking powder
- 5 g (1 tsp) baking soda
- 30 ml (2 tbsp) warm water
- 135 g (4.8 oz/1¼ cups) parmesan, grated
- 5 g (a pinch) of salt
- 385 g (13.5 oz/4 cups) almond flour
- 30 g (1 oz/2 tbsp) ghee, melted
- 80 ml (1/3 cup) almond milk
- 1 egg

Directions:

1. Add all of the ingredients to your bread machine carefully following the instructions of the manufacturer.
2. Set the program of your bread machine to Basic and set the crust type to light. Press START.
3. Cool the bread down, slice, and serve.

Nutritional Content
Calories: 100; Fat: 5 g; Carbs: 4 g; Protein: 4 g.

Pineapple Coconut Bread

Preparation Time: 10 minutes
Cooking Time: 2-4 hours
Servings: 12

Ingredients:

- 90 g (3.2 oz) butter, at room temperature
- 2 eggs, at room temperature
- 120 ml (½ cup) coconut milk, at room temperature
- 120 ml (½ cup) pineapple juice, at room temperature
- 235 g (8.3 oz) sugar
- 10 g (0.4 oz) coconut extract
- 470 g (16.6 oz) all-purpose flour
- 180 g (6.3 oz) shredded sweetened coconut
- 5 g (2 tbsps.) baking powder
- 5 g (½ tsp) salt

Directions:

1. Place the butter, eggs, coconut milk, pineapple juice, sugar, and coconut extract in your bread machine.
2. Select Quick/Rapid bread and press Start.
3. Stir together the flour, coconut, baking powder, and salt in a small bowl.
4. When the first fast mixing is done and the machine signals, add the dry ingredients.
5. Once the loaf is done, remove the bucket from the machine.
6. Let the loaf stand for 5 minutes.
7. Remove the loaf from bucket and put on a rack to cool.

Nutritional Content
Calories: 249; Protein: 3 g; Fat: 11 g; Carbs: 36 g

Flaxseed Bread

Preparation time: 10 minutes
Cooking time: 20 minutes
Servings: 6

Ingredients:

- 300 g (10.6 oz 2 cups) flaxseed, ground
- 5 g (1 tbsp) baking powder
- 200 g (7.1 oz/1½ cups) protein isolate
- 1 g (a pinch) salt
- 6 egg whites, whisked
- 1 egg, whisked
- 180 ml (¾ cup) water
- 45 ml (3 tbsp) coconut oil, melted
- 200 g (¼ cup) stevia

Directions:

1. Add all of the ingredients to your bread machine carefully following the instructions of the manufacturer.
2. Set the program of your bread machine to Basic and set the crust type to light. Press START.
3. Cool the bread down, slice, and serve.

Nutritional Content
Calories 263; Fat: 17 g; Carbs: 2 g; Protein: 20 g.

Orange Cranberry Bread

Preparation Time: 10 minutes
Cooking Time: 2-4 hours
Servings: 8

Ingredients:

- 175 ml milk, at 25°C (80°F)
- 175 g (6.2 oz) sugar
- 160 g (5.6 oz) melted butter, cooled
- 2 eggs, at room temperature
- 60 ml freshly squeezed orange juice, at room temperature
- 15 g (0.5 oz) orange zest
- 5 ml (2 tbsp) pure vanilla extract
- 530 g (18.7 oz) all-purpose flour
- 235 g (8.3 oz) sweetened dried cranberries
- 10 g (0.4 oz) baking powder
- 5 g (2 tbsp) baking soda
- 5 g (½ tsp) salt
- 1 g (1 tsp) ground nutmeg

Directions:

1. Add the milk, sugar, butter, eggs, orange juice, zest, and vanilla into your bread machine.
2. Select Quick/Rapid bread and press Start.
3. Stir the flour, cranberries, baking powder, baking soda, salt, and nutmeg in a medium bowl.
4. Add the dry ingredients after the first fast mixing is done and the machine signals.
5. Once the loaf is done, remove the bucket from the machine.
6. Let the loaf stand for 5 minutes.
7. Remove the loaf from bucket and put on a rack to cool.

Nutritional Content
Calories: 206; Protein: 4 g; Fat: 7 g; Carbs: 33 g

Broccoli and Cauliflower Bread

Preparation Time: 2 hours 20 minutes
Cooking Time: 50 minutes
Servings: 6

Ingredients:

- 235 ml (¼ cup) water
- 60 ml (4 tbsp) olive oil
- 1 egg white
- 5 ml (1 tsp) lemon juice
- 2/3 cup grated cheddar cheese
- 10 g (3 tbsp) green onion
- 80 g (2.8 oz/½ cup) broccoli, chopped
- 100 g (3.5 oz/½ cup) cauliflower, chopped
- 5 g (½ tsp) lemon pepper seasoning
- 240 g (240 oz/2 cups) bread flour
- 5 g (1 teaspoon) bread machine yeast

Directions:

1. Add all of the ingredients to your bread machine, carefully following the instructions of the manufacturer
2. Set the program of your bread machine to Basic/White Bread and set crust type to Medium
3. Press START
4. Wait until the cycle completes
5. Once the loaf is ready, take the bucket out and let the loaf cool for 5 minutes
6. Gently shake the bucket to remove the loaf
7. Transfer to a cooling rack, slice and serve

Nutritional Content
Calories: 156; Fat: 8 g; Carbs: 17 g; Protein: 5 g

Celery Bread

Preparation time: 2 hours and 10 minutes
Cooking time: 35 minutes
Servings: 6

Ingredients:

- 50 g (1.8 oz/½ cup) celery, chopped
- 100 g (3.5 oz/3 cups) almond flour
- 5g (1 tsp) baking soda
- 5 g (1 tsp) baking powder
- 30 ml (2 tbsp) coconut oil, melted
- 5 (a pinch) of salt
- 50 g (1.7 oz/½ cup) celery puree

Directions:

1. Add all of the ingredients to your bread machine, carefully following the instructions of the manufacturer
2. Set the program of your bread machine to Basic/White Bread and set crust type to Medium
3. Press START
4. Wait until the cycle completes
5. Once the loaf is ready, take the bucket out and let the loaf cool for 5 minutes
6. Gently shake the bucket to remove the loaf
7. Transfer to a cooling rack, slice and serve

Nutritional Content
Calories: 162; Fat: 6 g; Carbs: 6 g; Protein: 4 g

Lemon-Lime Blueberry Bread

Preparation Time: 10 minutes
Cooking Time: 2-4 hours
Servings: 12

Ingredients:

- 175 g (6 oz) plain yogurt, at room temperature
- 120 ml (½ cup) water, at 25°C (80°F)
- 45 ml (3 tbsps.) honey
- 15 g (0.5 oz) melted butter, cooled
- 5 g (½ tsp) salt
- 5 ml (1 tsp) lemon extract
- 5 g (1 tsp) lime zest
- 235 g (8.3 oz) dried blueberries
- 705 g (24.9 oz) white bread flour
- 10 g (0.4 oz) instant yeast

Directions:

1. Add the ingredients into your bread machine as per your manufacture's suggestions.
2. Select Basic/White bread and medium or light crust, and select Start button.
3. Once the loaf is done, remove the bucket from the machine.
4. Let the loaf stand for five minutes.
5. Remove the loaf from bucket and put on a rack to cool.

Nutritional Content
Calories: 159; Protein: 5 g; Fat: 2 g; Carbs: 31 g

Potato Bread

Preparation Time: 3 hours
Cooking Time: 45 minutes
Servings: 2 loaves

Ingredients:
- 5 g (1¾ tsp) active dry yeast
- 10 g (2 tbsp) dry milk
- 15 g (¼ cup) instant potato flakes
- 25 g (2 tbsps.) sugar
- 480 g (16.9 oz/4 cups) bread flour
- 5 g (1 tsp) salt
- 30 g (1.1 oz/2 tbsps.) butter
- 295 ml (1¼ cups) water

Directions:
1. Put all the liquid ingredients in the pan. Add all the dry ingredients, except the yeast. Form a shallow hole in the middle of the dry ingredients and place the yeast.
2. Secure the pan in the machine and close the lid. Choose the basic setting and your desired color of the crust. Press Start.
3. Allow the bread to cool before slicing.

Nutritional Content
Calories: 35; Carbs: 19 g; Fat: 0 g; Protein: 4 g

Minted Bread

Preparation Time: 2 hours
Cooking Time: 1 hour
Servings: 7

Ingredients:
- 5 g (1 tsp) yeast
- 180 g (6.3 oz/1½ cups) white bread flour
- 70 g (6 oz/½ cup) whole meal bread flour
- 5 g (½ tsp) fine sea salt
- 5 g (2 tbsps.) finely chopped fresh mint
- 350 ml (1½ cup) apple juice

Directions:
1. Add all the ingredients in the container in the correct order for your machine.
2. Fit the container into the bread machine and close the lid.
3. Select the basic white setting, medium crust, and the appropriate size. Press Start.
4. When the program has finished, lift the pan out of the machine, turn the bread out onto a wire rack and leave to cool completely.

Nutritional Content
Calories: 143; Fat: 1 g; Carbs: 23 g; Protein: 5 g

Apple Spice Bread

Preparation Time: 10 minutes
Cooking Time: 2-4 hours
Servings: 12

Ingredients:
- 235 ml milk, at 25°C (80°F)
- 40 g (1.1 oz) melted butter, cooled
- 30 g (1.1 oz) sugar
- 5 (½ tsp) g salt
- 5 g (1 tsp) ground cinnamon
- 5 g (Pinch) ground cloves
- 705 g (24.9 oz) white bread flour
- 10 g (2 tbsps.) dry yeast
- 235 g (8.3 oz) finely diced peeled apple

Directions:
1. Place the ingredients, except the apple, in your bread machine as per your manufacture's suggestions.
2. Select Basic/White bread, choose light or medium crust, and press Start.
3. When the machine signals, add the apple to the bucket or add it just before the end of the second kneading cycle if your machine does not have a signal.
4. Once the loaf is done, remove the bucket from the machine.
5. Let the loaf cool for five minutes.
6. Remove the loaf from bucket and put on a rack to cool.

Nutritional Content
Calories: 163; Protein: 4 g; Fat: 3 g; Carbs: 29 g

Coriander and Chili Bread

Preparation Time: 2 hours
Cooking Time: 40 minutes
Servings: 6

Ingredients:

- 5 g (1 tsp) yeast
- 180 g (6.3 oz/2½ cups) white bread flour
- 5 g (½ tsp) salt
- 160 ml (2/3 cup) coconut milk and water each
- 5 g (2) mild green chilies, seeds removed and finely chopped
- 10 g (a handful of) chopped fresh coriander

Directions:

1. Put all the ingredients, except for the chilies and coriander, into the pan in the correct order for your bread machine.
2. Fit the pan into the bread machine and close the lid.
3. Select the basic white raisin setting, medium crust, and the appropriate size. Press Start. When the machine indicates (with a beeping sound), add the chilies and coriander and close the lid again.
4. When the program has finished, lift the pan out of the machine, turn the bread out on to a wire rack and leave to cool completely.

Nutritional Content

Calories: 234; Protein: 8 g; Fat: 1 g; Carbs: 29 g

Peaches and Cream Bread

Preparation Time: 10 minutes
Cooking Time: 2-4 hours
Servings: 6

Ingredients:

- 180 g (6.3 oz) canned peaches, drained and chopped
- 80 g (2.8 oz) heavy whipping cream, at 80°F to 90°F
- 1 egg, at room temperature
- 15 g (0.5 oz) melted butter, cooled
- 35 g (1.5 oz) sugar
- 5 g (½ tsp) salt
- 5 g (1 tsp) ground cinnamon
- 1 g (½ tsp) ground nutmeg
- 80 g (2.8 oz) whole-wheat flour
- 630 g (22.2 oz) white bread flour
- 5 g (1 tsp) instant yeast

Directions:

1. Put the ingredients in your bread machine as per your manufacture's suggestions.
2. Select Basic/White bread and medium or light crust, and select Start button.
3. Once the loaf is done, remove the bucket from the machine.
4. Let the loaf stand for 5 minutes.
5. Remove the loaf from bucket and put on a rack to cool.

Nutritional Content
Calories: 153; Protein: 4 g; Fat: 3 g; Carbs: 27 g

Chapter 3: Buns and Bagels Recipes

Onion Buns

Preparation Time: 1 hour
Cooking Time: 1 hours
Servings: 10

Ingredients:
For dough:
- 3/5 cup (150 ml) water
- 15 ml (1 Tbsp) olive oil
- 250 g (9 oz/2 cups) all-purpose flour
- 10 g (1 Tbsp) fresh yeast
- 5 g (¼ tsp) salt
- 1 onion, diced
- 15 ml (1 Tbsp) olive oil

Directions:
1. Fry the onion in a pan with olive oil.
2. Knead the dough in a bread machine.
3. Once the machine beeps, add the fried onion.
4. Let the dough rest for 45 minutes.
5. Take the dough out of the bread maker.
6. Place it on a floured surface and divide it into 10 equal parts.
7. Shape buns from the ready-to-use dough.
8. Place the buns on a baking sheet covered with oiled paper, close to each other. Cover with a towel.
9. Leave the buns in a warm place for 30 minutes to rest and rise.
10. Preheat the oven to 200°C (400°F).
11. Bake until golden brown (about 15-20 minutes).

Nutritional Content
Calories: 321; Fat: 11.4 g; Carbs: 14.1 g; Protein: 10 g

Cottage Cheese Buns

Preparation Time: 1 hour
Cooking Time: 1 hour
Servings: 10

Ingredients:
For dough:
- 1/6 cup (40 ml) water
- 125 g (1 cup /4.4 oz) cottage cheese
- 2 tsp. (10 g) butter
- 250 g (2 cups/9 oz.) all-purpose flour
- 10 g (1 Tbsp). fresh yeast
- 3 g (¼ tsp) salt
- 5 g (1 tsp) sugar

Directions:
1. Knead the dough in a bread machine. Let it rest for 45 minutes.
2. Take the dough out of the bread maker.
3. Place it on a floured surface and divide it into 10 equal parts.
4. Shape buns from the ready-to-use dough.
5. Place the buns on a baking sheet covered with oiled parchment paper. Cover with a towel.
6. Leave the buns in a warm place for 30 minutes to rest and rise.
7. Preheat the oven to 200°C (400°F).
8. Bake until golden brown (about 15-20 minutes) and allow 20 minutes to cool.

Nutritional Content
Calories: 254; Fat: 9.4 g; Carbs: 23.1 g; Protein: 11 g

Bacon Buns

Preparation Time: 1 hour
Cooking Time: 1 hours
Servings: 10

Ingredients:
For dough:
- 3/5 cup (150 ml) water
- 1 Tbsp. (15 ml) olive oil
- 250 g (2 cups/ 9 oz.) all-purpose flour
- 9 g (1 Tbsp) fresh yeast
- 3 g (¼ tsp) salt
- 3½ oz (100 g) bacon, diced
- 15 ml (1 Tbsp) olive oil

Directions:
1. Fry the bacon in a pan with olive oil.
2. Knead the dough in a bread machine.
3. Once the machine beeps, add fried bacon.
4. Let the dough rest for 45 minutes.
5. Take the dough out of the bread maker.
6. Place it on a floured surface and divide it into 10 equal parts.
7. Shape buns from the ready-to-use dough.
8. Place them on a baking sheet covered with oiled parchment paper, close to each other. Cover with a towel.
9. Leave the buns in a warm place for 30 minutes to rest and rise.
10. Preheat the oven to 200°C (400°F).
11. Bake until golden brown (about 15-20 minutes).

Nutritional Content
Calories: 423; Fat: 9 g; Carbs: 23.1 g; Protein: 11 g

Olive Buns

Servings: 10
Preparation Time: 1 hour
Cooking Time: 1 hour

Ingredients:
For dough:
- 160 ml (2/3 cup) water
- 4 tsp. (20 ml) olive oil
- 250 g (9 oz/2 cups) all-purpose flour
- 5 g (1 Tbsp) fresh yeast
- 1 g (¼ tsp) salt
- 50 g (1.8 oz/¼ cup) green olives, chopped
- 50 g (1.8 oz/¼ cup) black olives, chopped
- 1 g (1 tsp) oregano

Directions:
1. Knead the dough in a bread machine. Once the machine beeps, add olives and oregano.
2. Let the dough rest for 45 minutes.
3. Take the dough out of the bread maker.
4. Place it on a floured surface and divide it into 10 equal parts.
5. Shape buns from the ready-to-use dough.
6. Place them on a baking sheet covered with oiled parchment paper. Cover with a towel.
7. Leave the buns in a warm place for 30 minutes to rest and rise.
8. Preheat the oven to 200°C (400°F).
9. Bake until golden brown (about 15-20 minutes).

Nutritional Content
Calories: 432; Fat: 10 g; Carbs: 14.1 g; Protein: 10 g

Lemon Buns

Preparation Time: 1 hour
Cooking Time: 1 hours
Servings: 10

Ingredients:

For dough:

- 150 m (2/3 cup l) water
- 10 ml (2 tsp.) olive oil
- 5 ml (1 tsp) lemon juice
- 250 g (2 cups / 9 oz.) all-purpose flour
- 10 g (1 Tbsp) fresh yeast
- 5 g (¼ tsp) salt
- 5 g (2 Tbsp) lemon zest, grated

Directions:

1. Knead the dough in a bread machine. Let it rest for 45 minutes.
2. Take the dough out of the bread maker.
3. Place the dough on a floured surface and divide it into 10 equal parts.
4. Shape buns from the ready-to-use dough.
5. Place them on a baking sheet covered with oiled parchment paper. Cover with a towel.
6. Leave the buns in a warm place for 30 minutes to rest and rise.
7. Preheat the oven to 200°C (400°F).
8. Bake until golden brown (about 15-20 minutes

Nutritional Content

Calories: 432; Fat: 13.4 g; Carbs: 28.3 g; Protein: 11 g

Whole-Grain Buns

Preparation Time: 1 hour
Cooking Time: 1 hour
Servings: 10

Ingredients:
For dough:
- 150 ml (3/5 cup) water
- 15 ml (1 Tbsp) olive oil
- 5 g (1 tsp) honey
- 2 cups (250 g/ 9 oz.) whole-grain flour
- 10 g (1 Tbsp) fresh yeast
- 5 g (¼ tsp) salt

Directions:
1. Knead the dough in a bread machine. Let it rest for 45 minutes.
2. Take the dough out of the bread maker.
3. Place the dough on a floured surface and divide it into 10 equal parts.
4. Shape buns from the ready-to-use dough.
5. Place them on a baking sheet covered with oiled parchment paper, close to each other. Cover with a towel.
6. Leave the buns in a warm place for 30 minutes to rest and rise.
7. Preheat the oven to 200°C (400°F).
8. Bake until golden brown (about 15-20 minutes).

Nutritional Content
Calories: 452; Fat: 15 g; Carbs: 12 g; Protein: 17 g

Fig Rosemary Buns

Preparation Time:+ Cooking Time: 2 hours
Servings: 10 buns

Ingredients:
For dough:
- 125 ml (½ cup) red wine
- 50 ml (1/5 cup) water
- 5 ml (1 Tbsp) olive oil
- 250 g (2 cups/9 oz) all-purpose flour
- 10 g (1 Tbsp) fresh yeast
- 5 g (¼ tsp) salt
- 5 g (1 tsp) rosemary, chopped

Directions:
1. Knead the dough in a bread machine.
2. Let the dough rest for 45 minutes.
3. Take the dough out of the bread maker.
4. Place it on a floured surface and divide it into 10 equal parts.
5. Shape buns from the ready-to-use dough.
6. Place them on a baking sheet covered with oiled parchment paper. Cover with a towel.
7. Leave the buns in a warm place for 30 minutes to rest and rise.
8. Preheat the oven to 200°C (400°F).
9. Bake until golden brown (about 15-20 minutes).

Nutritional Content
Calories: 322; Fat: 20.2 g; Carbs: 26.1 g; Protein: 27 g

Basil Buns

Preparation Time: 1 hour
Cooking Time: 1 hour
Servings: 10

Ingredients:
For dough:
- 150 ml (2/3 cup) water
- 10 ml (2 tsp.) olive oil
- 5 ml (1 tsp) lemon juice
- 250 g (2 cups / 9 oz.) all-purpose flour
- 10 g (1 Tbsp) fresh yeast
- 5 g (¼ tsp) salt
- 10 g (½ cup) fresh basil, finely chopped

Directions:
1. Knead the dough in a bread machine. Once the machine beeps, add chopped basil.
2. Let the dough rest for 45 minutes.
3. Take the dough out of the bread maker.
4. Place the dough on a floured surface and divide into 10 equal parts.
5. Shape buns from the ready-to-use dough.
6. Place them on a baking sheet covered with oiled parchment paper. Cover with a towel.
7. Leave the buns in a warm place for 30 minutes to rest and rise.
8. Preheat the oven to 200°C (400°F).
9. Bake until golden brown (about 15-20 minutes).

Nutritional Content
Calories: 321; Fat: 12.4 g; Carbs: 14.1 g; Protein: 10 g

Healthy Whole-Grain Bagels

Preparation Time: 1 hour
Cooking Time: 1 hour 20 minutes
Servings: 10

Ingredients:
For dough:
- 200 ml (4/5 cup) water
- 100 ml (2/5 cup) milk
- 20 g (1½ Tbsp.) butter
- 40 g (1 Tbsp.) honey
- 500 g (17.6 oz/3½ cup) whole-grain flour
- 10 g (1 Tbsp) fresh yeast
- 5 g (½ tsp) salt

For glaze:
- 85 g (6.5 oz/2 Tbsp) honey
- 1 egg yolk
- 1/5 cup (50 ml) milk
- 7 g (2.5 oz/1½ cup) sesame seeds

Directions:
1. Knead the dough in a bread machine. Let it rest for 45 minutes.
2. Roll ready-to-use dough into a cylinder and cut it into 10 equal slices. Shape a round bun out of each slice, slightly flatten it and make a hole in the center, increasing it to 1 inch (2-3 cm) in diameter.
3. Place them on a baking sheet covered with oiled parchment paper. Then let them rest and rise for 45 minutes.
4. Fill a large pan with water, add honey, and bring it to a boil.
5. Put each bagel in the boiling water for 30 seconds, remove, drain, and immediately dip one side of the bagel in sesame seeds. All the steps should be done quite fast, as the dough dries quickly, and the seeds might not stick to it. Place the bagels on a baking tray with their seeded side up.
6. Another way around is to take the bagels out of the boiling water and put them on a baking sheet. Then brush each bagel with some milk and egg yolk mixture and sprinkle with seeds.
7. Bake the bagels in a preheated oven at 200°C (400°F). If you prefer your bagels soft, bake them for 12 minutes. Set the baking time to 15 minutes if you like a harder version.
8. Allow to cool down on the grid.

Nutritional Content
Calories: 342; Fat: 21.4 g; Carbs: 23.4 g; Protein: 15 g

Sesame Savory Bagels

Preparation Time: 1 hour
Cooking Time: 1 hour 20 minutes
Servings: 10

Ingredients:

For dough:
- 200 ml (4/5 cup) water
- 100 ml (2/5 cup) milk
- 20 g (1½ Tbsp) butter
- 40 g (1.5 oz /1 Tbsp) honey
- 400 g (3 cups /13.5 oz.) all-purpose flour
- 90 g (2/3 cup / 3 oz.) wheat whole-grain flour
- 9 g (1 Tbsp) fresh yeast
- 5 g (½ tsp) salt
- 100 g (3.5 oz/20 tsp) sesame seeds

For glaze:
- 85 g (3.0 oz/2 Tbsp). honey
- 1 egg yolk
- 50 ml (1/5 cup) milk
- 36 g (1.3 oz/¼ cup) sesame seeds

Directions:
1. Knead the dough in a bread machine. Once the machine beeps, add sesame seeds.
2. Let the dough rest for 45 minutes.
3. Roll ready-to-use dough into a cylinder and cut it into 10 equal slices. Shape a round bun out of each slice, slightly flatten it and make a hole in the center, increasing it to 1 inch (2-3 cm) in diameter.
4. Place them on a baking sheet covered with oiled parchment paper. Then let them rest and rise for 45 minutes.
5. Fill a large pan with water, add honey, and bring it to a boil.
6. Put each bagel in the boiling water for 30 seconds, remove, drain, and immediately dip one side of the bagel in sesame seeds. All the steps should be done quite fast, as the dough dries quickly, and the seeds might not stick to it. Place the bagels on a baking tray with their seeded side up.
7. Another way around is to take the bagels out of the boiling water and put them on a baking sheet. Then brush each bagel with some milk and egg yolk mixture and sprinkle with seeds.
8. Bake the bagels in a preheated oven at 200°C (400°F). If you prefer your bagels soft, bake them for 12 minutes. Set the baking time to 15 minutes if you like a harder version.
9. Allow to cool down on the grid.

Nutritional Content
Calories: 313; Fat: 20.2 g; Carbs: 19.3 g; Protein: 16 g

Poppy Seed Bagels

Preparation Time: 1 hour
Cooking Time: 1 hour 20 minutes
Servings: 10

Ingredients:

For dough:
- 200 ml (4/5 cup) water
- 100 ml (2/5 cup) milk
- 20 g (1½ Tbsp) butter
- 40 g (1 Tbsp) honey
- 400 g (13.5 oz/3 cups.) all-purpose flour
- 90 g (2/3 cup / 3 oz.) wheat whole-grain flour
- 10 g (1 Tbsp) fresh yeast
- 5 g (½ tsp) salt
- 180 g (6.3 oz/20 tsp) poppy seeds

For glaze:
- 85 g (6.5 oz/2 Tbsp) honey
- 1 egg yolk
- 50 ml (1/5 cup) milk
- 20 g (2 tsp) poppy seeds

Directions:

1. Knead the dough in a bread machine. Once the machine beeps, add poppy seeds.
2. Let the dough rest for 45 minutes.
3. Roll ready-to-use dough into a cylinder and cut it into 10 equal slices. Shape a round bun out of each slice, slightly flatten it and make a hole in the center, increasing it to 1 inch (2-3 cm) in diameter.
4. Place them on a baking sheet covered with oiled parchment paper. Then let them rest and rise for 45 minutes.
5. Fill a large pan with water, add honey, and bring it to a boil.
6. Put each bagel in the boiling water for 30 seconds, remove, drain, and immediately dip one side of the bagel in poppy seeds. All the steps should be done quite fast, as the dough dries quickly, and the seeds might not stick to it. Place the bagels on a baking tray with their seeded side up.
7. Another way around is to take the bagels out of the boiling water and put them on a baking sheet. Then brush each bagel with some milk and egg yolk mixture and sprinkle with seeds.
8. Bake the bagels in a preheated oven at 200°C (400°F). If you prefer your bagels soft, bake them for 12 minutes. Set the baking time to 15 minutes if you like a harder version.
9. Allow to cool down on the grid.

Nutritional Content
Calories: 330; Carbs: 70g; Fat: 2g; Protein: 11g

Cumin Bagels

Servings: 10 bagels
Preparation Time: 1 hour
Cooking Time: 1 hour 20 minutes

Ingredients:

- 200 ml (4/5 cup) water
- 100 ml (2/5 cup) milk
- 20 g (1½ Tbsp) butter
- 20 g (1 Tbsp) honey
- 400 g (3 cups /13½ oz.) all-purpose flour
- 90 g (2/3 cup /3 oz.) whole-grain flour
- 10 g (1 Tbsp) fresh yeast
- 5 g (½ tsp) salt
- 40 g (20 tsp) cumin

For glaze:

- 85 g (6.5 oz/2 Tbsp). honey
- 1 egg yolk
- 50 ml (1/5 cup) milk
- 10 g (2 tbsp) cumin seeds

Directions:

1. Knead the dough in a bread machine. Once the machine beeps, add cumin.
2. Let the dough rest for 45 minutes.
3. Roll ready-to-use dough into a cylinder and cut it into 10 equal slices. Shape a round bun out of each slice, slightly flatten it and make a hole in the center, increasing it to 1 inch (2-3 cm) in diameter.
4. Place them on a baking sheet covered with oiled parchment paper. Then let it rest and rise for 45 minutes.
5. Fill a large pan with water, add honey, and bring it to a boil.
6. Put each bagel in the boiling water for 30 seconds, remove, drain, and immediately dip one side of the bagel in cumin. All the steps should be done quite fast, as the dough dries quickly, and the cumin might not stick to it. Place the bagels on a baking tray with their seeded side up.
7. Another way around is to take the bagels out of the boiling water and put them on a baking sheet. Then brush each bagel with some milk and egg yolk mixture, and then sprinkle with cumin.
8. Bake the bagels in a preheated oven at 200°C (400°F). If you prefer your bagels soft, bake them for 12 minutes. Set the baking time to 15 minutes if you like a harder version.
9. Allow to cool down on the grid.

Nutritional Content
Calories: 427; Fat: 33 g; Carbs: 22 g; Protein: 17 g

Herb Savory Bagels

Servings: 10 bagels
Preparation Time: 1 hour
Cooking Time: 1 hour 20 minutes

Ingredients:

- 200 ml (4/5 cup) water
- 100 ml (2/5 cup) milk
- 20 g (1½ Tbsp) butter
- 20 g (1 Tbsp) honey
- 400 g (13½ oz/3 cups) all-purpose flour
- 90 g (3 oz/2/3 cup) whole-grain flour
- 10 g (1 Tbsp) fresh yeast
- 5 g (½ tsp) salt
- 20 g (10 tsp) herbs (oregano/rosemary/basil/etc.)

For glaze:

- 85 g (6.5 oz/2 Tbsp). honey
- 1 egg yolk
- 50 ml (1/5 cup) milk
- 10 g (2 tbsp) dry herbs

Directions:

1. Knead the dough in a bread machine. Once the machine beeps, add herbs.
2. Let the dough rest for 45 minutes.
3. Roll ready-to-use dough into a cylinder and cut it into 10 equal slices. Shape a round bun out of each slice, slightly flatten it and make a hole in the center, increasing it to 1 inch (2-3 cm) in diameter.
4. Place them on a baking sheet covered with oiled parchment paper. Then let it rest and rise for 45 minutes.
5. Fill a large pan with water, add honey, and bring it to a boil.
6. Put each bagel in the boiling water for 30 seconds, remove, drain, and immediately dip one side of the bagel in herbs. All the steps should be done quite fast, as the dough dries quickly, and the herbs might not stick to it. Place the bagels on a baking tray with their seeded side up.
7. Another way around is to take the bagels out of the boiling water and put them on a baking sheet. Then brush each bagel with some milk and egg yolk mixture and sprinkle with herbs.
8. Bake the bagels in a preheated oven at 200°C (400°F). If you prefer your bagels soft, bake them for 12 minutes. Set the baking time to 15 minutes if you like a harder version.
9. Allow to cool down on the grid.

Nutritional Content

Calories: 320; Fat: 5 g; Carbs: 44.2 g; Protein: 11 g

Chili Savory Bagels

Servings: 10 bagels
Preparation Time: 1 hour
Cooking Time: 1 hour 20 minutes

Ingredients:
- 200 ml (4/5 cup) water
- 100 ml (2/5 cup) milk
- 20 g (1½ Tbsp) butter
- 20 g (1 Tbsp) honey
- 400 g (13½ oz/3 cups) all-purpose flour
- 90 g (3 oz/2/3 cup.) whole-grain flour
- 10 g (1 Tbsp) fresh yeast
- 3 g (½ tsp) salt
- 20 g (10 tsp) chili powder

For glaze:
- 2 Tbsp. honey
- 1 egg yolk
- 1/5 cup (50 ml) milk

Directions:
1. Knead the dough in a bread machine. Once the machine beeps, add chili.
2. Let the dough rest for 45 minutes.
3. Roll ready-to-use dough into a cylinder and cut it into 10 equal slices. Shape a round bun out of each slice, slightly flatten it and make a hole in the center, increasing it to 1 inch (2-3 cm) in diameter.
4. Place them on a baking sheet covered with oiled parchment paper. Then let it rest and rise for 45 minutes.
5. Fill a large pan with water, add honey, and bring it to a boil.
6. Put each bagel in the boiling water for 30 seconds, remove, drain, and immediately dip one side of the bagel in the glaze. All the steps should be done quite fast, as the dough dries quickly, and the glaze might not stick to it. Place the bagels on a baking tray with their glazed side up.
7. Another way around is to take the bagels out of the boiling water and put them on a baking sheet. Then brush each bagel with some milk and egg yolk mixture, and then sprinkle with your favorite topping.
8. Bake the bagels in a preheated oven at 200°C (400°F). If you prefer your bagels soft, bake them for 12 minutes. Set the baking time to 15 minutes if you like a harder version.
9. Allow to cool down on the grid.

Nutritional Content
Calories: 300; Fat: 8.2 g; Carbs: 33 g; Protein: 10 g

Onion Bagels

Preparation Time: 1 hour
Cooking Time: 1 hours 20 minutes
Servings: 10

Ingredients:

- 200 ml cup (4/5) water
- 100 ml (2/5 cup) milk
- 20 g (1½ Tbsp) butter
- 20 g (1½ Tbsp) honey
- 400 g (13½ oz/3 cups.) all-purpose flour
- 90 g (3 oz/ 2/3 cup.) whole-grain flour
- 10 g (1 Tbsp) fresh yeast
- 5 g (½ tsp) salt
- 2 onions, finely chopped
- 5 ml (1 Tbsp) olive oil

For glaze:

- 85 g (6.5 oz/2 Tbsp). honey
- 1 egg yolk
- 50 ml (1/5 cup) milk

Directions:

1. Roast the chopped onion.
2. Knead the dough in a bread machine. Once the machine beeps, add the roasted onion.
3. Let the dough rest for 45 minutes.
4. Roll ready-to-use dough into a cylinder and cut it into 10 equal slices. Shape a round bun out of each slice, slightly flatten it and make a hole in the center, increasing it to 1 inch (2-3 cm) in diameter.
5. Place them on a baking sheet covered with oiled parchment paper. Then let them rest and rise for 45 minutes.
6. Combine and slightly blend the glaze mixture.
7. Before baking, brush each bagel with icing.
8. Bake the bagels in the preheated oven at 200°C (400°F). If you prefer your bagels soft, bake them for 12 minutes. Set the baking time to 15 minutes if you like their harder version.
9. Allow to cool down on the grid.

Nutritional Content
Calories: 230; Carbs: 48g; Fat: 1g; Protein: 8g

Cheese Bagels

Preparation Time:
Cooking Time: 2 hours 20 minutes
Servings: 10

Ingredients:
- 200 ml (4/5 cup) water
- 100 ml (2/5 cup) milk
- 20 g (1½ Tbsp) butter
- 20 g (1½ Tbsp) honey
- 400 g (13½ oz/3 cups) all-purpose flour
- 90 g (3 oz/2/3 cup) whole-grain flour
- 10 g (1 Tbsp) fresh yeast
- 5 g (½ tsp) salt
- 100 g (3.5 oz/1 cup) parmesan, grated

For topping:
- 75 g (2.5 oz/¾ cup) parmesan, grated

Directions:
1. Knead the dough in a bread machine. Once the machine beeps, add grated cheese.
2. Let the dough rest for 45 minutes.
3. Roll ready-to-use dough into a cylinder and cut it into 10 equal slices. Shape a round bun out of each slice, slightly flatten it and make a hole in the center, increasing it to 1 inch (2-3 cm) in diameter.
4. Place them on a baking sheet covered with oiled parchment paper. Then let them rest and rise for 45 minutes.
5. Before baking, sprinkle each bagel with grated cheese.
6. Bake the bagels in a preheated oven at 200°C (400°F). If you prefer your bagels soft, bake them for 12 minutes. Set the baking time to 15 minutes if you like a harder version.
7. Allow to cool down on the grid.

Nutritional Content
Calories: 276; Carbs: 49g; Fat: 3.7g; Protein: 10.6g

Herbed Buns

Preparation time: 10 minutes
Cooking time: 3 hours 30 minutes
Servings: 6

Ingredients:

- 30 g (1 oz/¼ cup) arrowroot flour
- 35 g (1.3 oz/ 1/3 cup) coconut flour
- 5 g (1 tsp) baking powder
- 1 g (¼ tsp) garlic powder
- 1 g (¼ tsp) dried parsley
- 1 g (¼ tsp) oregano
- 1 g (¼ tsp) dried basil
- 55 g (1.9 oz/¼ cup) butter, melted

Directions:

1. Put all of the ingredients to the pan o the Bread Machine (except melted butter).
2. Set the program to "Dough" cycle and let the cycle run.
3. Remove the dough (using lightly floured hands) and carefully place it on a floured surface.
4. Cover with a light film/cling paper and let the dough rise for 10 minutes.
5. Take a large cookie sheet and grease with butter.
6. Cut the risen dough into 15-20 pieces and shape them into balls.
7. Place the balls onto the sheet (2 inches apart) and cover.
8. Place in a warm place and let them rise for 30-40 minutes until the dough doubles.
9. Preheat oven to 190°C (375°F), transfer the cookie sheet to your oven and bake for 12-15 minutes.
10. Brush the top with a bit of butter, enjoy!

Nutritional Content
Calories: 152; Carbs: 9g; Fat: 2g; Protein: 4.2g

Apricot Bagels

Preparation Time: 1 hour
Cooking Time: 1 hour 20 minutes
Servings: 10

Ingredients:

- 200 ml (4/5 cup) water
- 100 ml (2/5 cup) milk
- 20 g (1½ Tbsp) butter
- 20 g (1½ Tbsp) honey
- 400 g (13½ oz/3 cups) all-purpose flour
- 2/3 cup (90 g, 3 oz.) whole-grain flour
- 10 g (1 Tbsp) fresh yeast
- 5 g (½ tsp) salt
- 600 g (21 oz) 4 dried apricots, finely chopped

For glaze:

- 85 g (6.5 oz/2 Tbsp). honey
- 1 egg yolk
- 1/5 cup (50 ml) milk
- 20 g (2 tbsp) sunflower seeds

Directions:

1. Knead the dough in a bread machine. Once the machine beeps, add dried apricots.
2. Let the dough rest for 45 minutes.
3. Roll ready-to-use dough into a cylinder and cut it into 10 equal slices. Shape a round bun out of each slice, slightly flatten it and make a hole in the center, increasing it to 1 inch (2-3 cm) in diameter.
4. Place them on a baking sheet covered with oiled parchment paper. Then let them rest and rise for 45 minutes.
5. Fill a large pan with water, add honey, and bring it to a boil.
6. Put each bagel in the boiling water for 30 seconds, remove, drain, and immediately dip one side of the bagel in sunflower seeds. All the steps should be done quite fast, as the dough dries quickly, and the seeds might not stick to it. Place the bagels on a baking tray with their seeded side up.
7. Another way around is to take the bagels out of the boiling water and put them on a baking sheet. Then brush each bagel with some milk and egg yolk mixture, sprinkle with sunflower seeds.
8. Bake the bagels in a preheated oven at 200°C (400°F). If you prefer your bagels soft, bake them for 12 minutes. Set the baking time to 15 minutes if you like a harder version.
9. Allow to cool down on the grid.

Nutritional Content

Calories: 244; Carbs: 36g; Fat: 2g; Protein: 11,2g

Chocolate Bagels

Preparation Time: 1 hour
Cooking Time: 1 hour 20 minutes
Servings: 10

Ingredients:
- 200 ml (4/5 cup) water
- 100 ml (2/5 cup) milk
- 20 g (1½ Tbsp) butter
- 43 g (1.5 o/z1½ Tbsp) honey
- 400 g (13½ oz/3 cups) all-purpose flour
- 90 g (3 oz/2/3 cup) whole-grain flour
- 10 g (1 Tbsp) fresh yeast
- 5 g (½ tsp) salt
- 15 g (10 tsp) chocolate drops

For glaze:
- 85 g (6.5 oz/2 Tbsp). honey
- 1 egg yolk
- 50 ml (1/5 cup) milk
- 100 g (3.5oz) Sesame seeds

Directions:
1. Knead the dough in a bread machine. Once the machine beeps, add chocolate.
2. Let the dough rest for 45 minutes.
3. Roll ready-to-use dough into a cylinder and cut it into 10 equal slices. Shape a round bun out of each slice, slightly flatten it and make a hole in the center, increasing it to 1 inch (2-3 cm) in diameter.
4. Place them on a baking sheet covered with oiled parchment paper. Then let them rest and rise for 45 minutes.
5. Fill a large pan with water, add honey, and bring it to a boil.
6. Put each bagel in the boiling water for 30 seconds; take it out of the water, drain and immediately dip one side of the bagel in sesame seeds. All the steps shall be done quite fast, as the dough dries quickly, and the sesame seeds might not stick to it. Place the bagels on a baking tray with their seeded side up.
7. Another way around is to take the bagels out of the boiling water and put them on a baking sheet. Then brush each bagel with some milk and egg yolk mixture and sprinkle with sesame seeds.
8. Bake the bagels in the preheated oven at 200°C (400°F). If you prefer your bagels soft, bake them for 12 minutes. Set the baking time to 15 minutes if you like their harder version.
9. Allow to cool down on the grid.

Nutritional Content
Calories: 290; Carbs: 58g; Fat: 2.5g; Protein: 10g

Citrus Bagels

Preparation Time: 1 hour
Cooking Time: 1 hour 20 minutes
Servings: 10

Ingredients:
- 200 ml (4/5 cup) water
- 100 ml (2/5 cup) milk
- 20 g (1½ Tbsp) butter
- 20 g (1½ Tbsp) honey
- 400 g (13½ oz/3 cups) all-purpose flour

For glaze:
- 85 g (6.5 oz/2 Tbsp). honey
- 1 egg yolk
- 50 ml (1/5 cup) milk
- 90 g (3 oz/ 2/3 cup) whole-grain flour
- 10 g (1 Tbsp) fresh yeast
- 5 g (½ tsp) salt
- 20 g (10 tsp) zest (lemon, orange, etc.), finely grated
- 100 g (3.5oz) sunflower seeds/sesame seeds/poppy seeds

Directions:
1. Knead the dough in a bread machine. Once the machine beeps, add grated zest.
2. Let the dough rest for 45 minutes.
3. Roll ready-to-use dough into a cylinder and cut it into 10 equal slices. Shape a round bun out of each slice, slightly flatten it and make a hole in the center, increasing it to 1 inch (2-3 cm) in diameter.
4. Place them on a baking sheet covered with oiled parchment paper. Then let them rest and rise for 45 minutes.
5. Fill a large pan with water, add honey, and bring it to a boil.
6. Put each bagel in the boiling water for 30 seconds, remove, drain, and immediately dip one side of the bagel in seeds. All the steps should be done quite fast, as the dough dries quickly, and the seeds might not stick to it. Place the bagels on a baking tray with their seeded side up.
7. Another way around is to take the bagels out of the boiling water and put them on a baking sheet. Then brush each bagel with some milk and egg yolk mixture and sprinkle with seeds.
8. Bake the bagels in a preheated oven at 200°C (400°F). If you prefer your bagels soft, bake them for 12 minutes. Set the baking time to 15 minutes if you like a harder version.
9. Allow to cool down on the grid.

Nutritional Content
Calories: 282; Carbs: 23g; Fat: 3g; Protein: 11g

Raisin Bagels

Preparation Time: 1 hour
Cooking Time: 1 hour 20 minutes
Servings: 10

Ingredients:
- 200 ml (4/5 cup) water
- 100 ml (2/5 cup) milk
- 20 g 1 (½ Tbsp) butter
- 20 g 1 (½ Tbsp) honey
- 400 g (13½ oz/3 cups) all-purpose flour
- 90 g (3 oz/2/3 cup) whole-grain flour
- 10 g (1 Tbsp) fresh yeast
- 5 g (½ tsp) salt
- 115 g (4 oz/¾ cup) raisins

For glaze:
- 85 g (6.5 oz/2 Tbsp). honey
- 1 egg yolk
- 50 ml (1/5 cup) milk

Directions:
1. Knead the dough in a bread machine. Once the machine beeps, add raisins.
2. Let the dough rest for 45 minutes.
3. Roll ready-to-use dough into a cylinder and cut it into 10 equal slices. Shape a round bun out of each slice, slightly flatten it and make a hole in the center, increasing it to 1 inch (2-3 cm) in diameter.
4. Place them on a baking sheet covered with oiled parchment paper. Then let them rest and rise for 45 minutes.
5. Combine the glaze ingredients and slightly whip.
6. Before baking, brush each bagel with the icing.
7. Bake the bagels in a preheated oven at 200°C (400°F). If you prefer your bagels soft, bake them for 12 minutes. Set the baking time to 15 minutes if you like a harder version.
8. Allow to cool down on the grid.

Nutritional Content
Calories: 230; Carbs: 47g; Fat: 2g; Protein: 10g

Coconut Bagels

Preparation Time: 1 hour
Cooking Time: 1 hour 20 minutes
Servings: 10

Ingredients:

- 200 ml (4/5 cup) water
- 100 ml (2/5 cup) milk
- 20 g (1½ Tbsp) butter
- 40 g (1.4 oz/1½ Tbsps.) honey
- 400 g (13½ oz/3 cups) all-purpose flour
- 90 g (3 oz/2/3 cup) whole-grain flour
- 10 g (1 Tbsp) fresh yeast
- 5 g (½ tsp) salt
- 115 g (4 oz/¾ cup) coconut chips

For glaze:

- 85 g (6.5 oz/2 Tbsp). honey
- 1 egg yolk
- 50 ml (1/5 cup) milk

Directions:

1. Knead the dough in a bread machine. Once the machine beeps, add coconut chips.
2. Let the dough rest for 45 minutes.
3. Roll ready-to-use dough into a cylinder and cut it into 10 equal slices. Shape a round bun out of each slice, slightly flatten it and make a hole in the center, increasing it to 1 inch (2-3 cm) in diameter.
4. Place them on a baking sheet covered with oiled parchment paper. Then let them rest and rise for 45 minutes.
5. Combine the glaze ingredients and slightly whip.
6. Before baking, brush each bagel with the icing.
7. Bake the bagels in a preheated oven at 200°C (400°F). If you prefer your bagels soft, bake them for 12 minutes. Set the baking time to 15 minutes if you like a harder version.
8. Allow to cool down on the grid.

Nutritional Content

Calories: 322; Carbs: 36; Fat: 7g; Protein: 11g

Nut Bagels

Preparation Time: 1 hour
Cooking Time: 1 hour 20 minutes
Servings: 10

Ingredients:
- 200 ml (4/5 cup) water
- 100 ml (2/5 cup) milk
- 20 g (1½ Tbsp) butter
- 20 g (1½ Tbsp) honey
- 400 g (3 cup /13½ oz) all-purpose flour
- 90 g (3 oz/ 2/3 cup) whole-grain flour
- 10 g (1 Tbsp) fresh yeast
- 5 g (½ tsp) salt
- 25 g (10 tsp) hazelnuts, chopped

For glaze:
- 85 g (6.5 oz/2 Tbsp). honey
- 1 egg yolk
- 50 ml (1/5 cup) milk

Directions:
1. Knead the dough in a bread machine. Once the machine beeps, add nuts.
2. Let the dough rest for 45 minutes.
3. Roll ready-to-use dough into a cylinder and cut it into 10 equal slices. Shape a round bun out of each slice, slightly flatten it and make a hole in the center, increasing it to 1 inch (2-3 cm) in diameter.
4. Place them on a baking sheet covered with oiled parchment paper. Then let them rest and rise for 45 minutes.
5. Fill a large pan with water, add honey, and bring it to a boil.
6. Put each bagel in the boiling water for 30 seconds, remove, drain, and immediately dip one side of the bagel in seeds. All the steps should be done quickly, as the dough dries quickly, and the seeds might not stick to it. Place the bagels on a baking tray with their seeded side up.
7. Another way around is to take the bagels out of the boiling water and put them on a baking sheet. Then brush each bagel with some milk and egg yolk mixture and sprinkle with seeds.
8. Bake the bagels in a preheated oven at 200°C (400°F). If you prefer your bagels soft, bake them for 12 minutes. Set the baking time to 15 minutes if you like a harder version.
9. Allow to cool down on the grid.

Nutritional Content
Calories: 330; Carbs: 55g; Fat: 3.5g; Protein: 11g

Chapter 4: Keto Bread Recipes

Yeast Bread

Preparation Time: 10 minutes
Cooking Time: 4 hours
Servings: 12 slices

Ingredients:

- 20 g (0.5 oz/2 teaspoons) dry yeast
- ½ teaspoon + 1 tablespoon erythritol sweetener, divided
- 300 ml (10 oz/1 ¼ cups) warm water, at 38°C (100°F)
- 45 ml (3 tbsp) avocado oil
- oz (1 cup/100 g) almond flour
- 1.2 oz (¼ cup/35 g) oat fiber
- 3.5 oz (¾ cup/100 g) soy flour
  - oz (½ cup/65 g) ground flax meal
- 10 g (1½ tsp) baking powder
- 5 g (½ tsp) salt

Directions:

1. Gather all the ingredients for the bread and plug in the bread machine having the capacity of 2 pounds of the bread recipe.
2. Pour water into the bread bucket, stir in ½ teaspoon sugar and yeast and let it rest for 10 minutes until emulsified.
3. Meanwhile, take a large bowl, place the remaining ingredients in it, and stir until mixed.
4. Pour flour mixture over the yeast mixture in the bread bucket, shut the lid, select the "basic/white" cycle or "low-carb" setting, and then press the up/down arrow button to adjust the baking time according to your bread machine; it will take 3 to 4 hours.
5. Press the crust button to select light crust if available, and press the "start/stop" button to switch on the bread machine.
6. When the bread machine beeps, open the lid, take out the bread basket, and lift out the bread.
7. Let the bread cool on a wire rack for 1 hour, then cut it into twelve slices and serve.

Nutritional Content
Calories: 163; Carbs: 24g; Fat: 6g; Protein: 3g

Keto Bread

Preparation Time: 10 minutes
Cooking Time: 30 minutes
Servings: 20

Ingredients:

- 145 g (5 oz/1 ½ cup) almond flour
- 2 tsp (6 drops) liquid stevia
- 5 g (1 pinch) pink Himalayan salt
- 1 g (¼ tsp) cream of tartar
- 10 g (3 tsp) baking powder
- 60 g (2 oz/¼ cup) butter, melted
- 30 g (1 oz/2 tbsp) Ghee
- 6 large eggs, separated

Directions:

1. In a bowl, to the egg whites, add cream of tartar and beat until soft peaks are formed.
2. Into another bowl, combine stevia, salt, baking powder, almond flour, melted butter. Mix well.
3. Grease the machine loaf pan with ghee.
4. Following the instructions on your machine's manual, mix the dry ingredients into the wet ingredients and pour in the bread machine loaf pan, taking care to follow how to mix them in the baking powder.
5. Place the bread pan in the machine, and select the basic bread setting, together with the bread size and crust type, if available, then press start once you have closed the lid of the machine.
6. When the bread is ready, remove the bread pan from the machine.
7. Let it cool before slicing.

Nutritional Content
Calories: 110; Carbs: 18g; Fat: 12g; Protein: 10g

Cream Cheese Bread

Preparation Time: 10 minutes
Cooking Time: 4 hours
Servings: 12 slices

Ingredients:
- ¼ cup (60 g/2.1 oz) butter, grass-fed, unsalted
- 1 cup and 3 tablespoons (140 g/5 oz) cream cheese, softened
- 4 egg yolks, pasteurized
- 5 g (1 tsp) vanilla extract, unsweetened
- 10 g (1 tsp) baking powder
- 5 g (¼ tsp) sea salt
- 5 g (2 tbsp) monk fruit powder
- 65 g (½ cup /2.3oz) peanut flour

Directions:
1. Gather all the ingredients for the bread and plug in the bread machine having the capacity of 2 pounds of the bread recipe.
2. Take a large bowl, place butter in it, beat in cream cheese until thoroughly combined, and then beat in egg yolks, vanilla, baking powder, salt, and monk fruit powder until well combined.
3. Add the egg mixture into the bread bucket, top with flour, shut the lid, select the "basic/white" cycle or "low-carb" setting, and then press the up/down arrow button to adjust baking time according to your bread machine; it will take 3 to 4 hours.
4. Press the crust button to select light crust if available, and press the "start/stop" button to switch on the bread machine.
5. When the bread machine beeps, open the lid, take out the bread basket, and lift out the bread.
6. Let the bread cool on a wire rack for 1 hour, then cut it into twelve slices and serve.

Nutritional Content
Calories: 150; Carbs: 24g; Fat: 5g; Protein: 3sg

Almond flour bread

Preparation time: 4 minutes
Cooking Time: 4 hours
Servings: 10 slices

Ingredients:

- 4 egg whites
- 2 egg yolks
- 190 g (6.7 oz/2 cups) almond flour
- 60 g (2 oz/¼ cup) butter, melted
- 10 g (2 tbsp) psyllium husk powder
- 5 g (1 ½ tsp) baking powder
- 1 g (½ tsp) xanthan gum
- 5 g (½ tsp) Salt
- 100 ml (½ cup) + 30 ml (2 tbsps.) warm water
- 5 g (2 ¼ tsp) yeast

Directions:

1. Use a small mixing bowl to combine all dry ingredients, except for the yeast.
2. In the bread machine pan add all wet ingredients.
3. Add all of your dry ingredients, from the small mixing bowl, in the bread machine pan. Top with the yeast.
4. Set the bread machine to the basic bread setting.
5. When the bread is done, remove bread machine pan from the bread machine.
6. Let cool slightly before transferring to a cooling rack.
7. The bread can be stored for up to 4 days on the counter and for up to 3 months in the freezer.

Nutritional Content
Calories 110; Carbs: 2.4 g; Fats 10 g; Protein 4 g

Cauliflower and Garlic Bread

Preparation Time: 10 minutes
Cooking Time: 4 hours
Servings: 9 slices

Ingredients:

- 5 eggs, pasteurized, separated
- 85 g (2/3 cup /3 oz) coconut flour
- 300 g (1½ cup /10.5 oz) riced cauliflower
- 5 g (1 tsp) minced garlic
- 5 g (½ tsp) sea salt
- 5 g (½ tbsp) chopped rosemary
- 5 g ½ tablespoon chopped parsley
- 10 g (¾ tbsp) baking powder
- 40 g (1.5 oz/3 tbsp) melted butter, grass-fed, unsalted

Directions:

1. Gather all the ingredients for the bread and plug in the bread machine having the capacity of 2 pounds of the bread recipe.
2. Take a medium bowl, place cauliflower rice in it, cover with a plastic wrap, and then microwave for 3 to 4 minutes until steamed.
3. Then drain the cauliflower, wrap in cheesecloth, and twist it well to squeeze out moisture as much as possible, set aside until required.
4. Place egg whites in a large bowl and whisk by using an electric whisker until stiff peaks form.
5. Then transfer one-fourth of whipped egg whites into a food for, add the remaining ingredients except for cauliflower and pulse for 2 minutes until blended.
6. Add cauliflower rice, pulse for 2 minutes until well combined, and then pulse in the remaining egg whites until just mixed.
7. Add batter into the bread bucket, shut the lid, select the "basic/white" cycle or "low-carb" setting, and then press the up/down arrow button to adjust baking time according to your bread machine; it will take 3 to 4 hours.
8. Press the crust button to select light crust if available, and press the "start/stop" button to switch on the bread machine.
9. When the bread machine beeps, open the lid, take out the bread basket, and lift out the bread.
10. Let the bread cool on a wire rack for 1 hour, then cut it into nine slices and serve.

Nutritional Content
Calories: 117; Carbs: 11g; Fat: 2g; Protein: 5g

Almond Meal Bread

Preparation Time: 10 minutes
Cooking Time: 4 hours
Servings: 10 slices

Ingredients:
- 4 eggs, pasteurized
- 60 ml (¼ cup) melted coconut oil
- 5 ml (1 tbsp) apple cider vinegar
- 215 g (2¼ cups) almond meal
- 5 g (1 tsp) baking soda
- 35 g (¼ cup) ground flaxseed meal
- 5 g (1 tsp) onion powder
- 5 g (1 tbsp) minced garlic
- 5 g (¼ tsp) sea salt
- 5 g (1 tsp) chopped sage leaves
- 1 g (1 tsp) fresh thyme
- 5 g (1 tsp) chopped rosemary leaves

Directions:
1. Gather all the ingredients for the bread and plug in the bread machine having the capacity of 2 pounds of the bread recipe.
2. Take a large bowl, crack eggs in it, and then beat in coconut oil and vinegar until well blended.
3. Take a separate large bowl, place the almond meal in it, add remaining ingredients, and stir until well mixed.
4. Add the egg mixture into the bread bucket, top with flour mixture, shut the lid, select the "basic/white" cycle or "low-carb" setting, and then press the up/down arrow button to adjust baking time according to your bread machine; it will take 3 to 4 hours.
5. Press the crust button to select light crust if available, and press the "start/stop" button to switch on the bread machine.
6. When the bread machine beeps, open the lid, take out the bread basket, and lift out the bread.
7. Let the bread cool on a wire rack for 1 hour, then cut it into ten slices and serve.

Nutritional Content
Calories: 172; Carbs: 16g; Fat: 2g; Protein: 7g

Macadamia Nut Bread

Preparation Time: 10 minutes
Cooking Time: 4 hours
Servings: 8

Ingredients:
- 135 g (4.8 oz/1 cup) macadamia nuts
- 5 eggs, pasteurized
- 10 ml (½ tsp) apple cider vinegar
- 30 g (1 oz/¼ cup) coconut flour
- 9 g (½ teaspoon) baking soda

Directions:
1. Gather all the ingredients for the bread and plug in the bread machine having the capacity of 1 pound of the bread recipe.
2. Place nuts in a blender, pulse for 2 to 3 minutes until mixture reaches a consistency of butter, and then blend in eggs and vinegar until smooth.
3. Stir in flour and baking soda until well mixed.
4. Add the batter into the bread bucket, shut the lid, select the "basic/white" cycle or "low-carb" setting, and then press the up/down arrow button to adjust baking time according to your bread machine; it will take 3 to 4 hours.
5. Press the crust button to select light crust if available, and press the "start/stop" button to switch on the bread machine.
6. When the bread machine beeps, open the lid, take out the bread basket, and lift out the bread.
7. Let the bread cool on a wire rack for 1 hour, then cut it into eight slices and serve.

Nutritional Content
Calories: 220; Carbs: 28g; Fat: 9g; Protein: 3g

Keto Breakfast Bread

Preparation Time: 15 minutes
Cooking Time: 40 minutes
Servings: 16 slices

Ingredients:

- 6 g (½ tsp) xanthan gum
- 3 g (½ tsp) salt
- 20 ml (2 tbsp) coconut oil
- 115 g (4 oz/½ cup) butter, melted
- 4 g (1 tsp) baking powder
- 190 g (6.7 oz) 2 cups of almond flour
- 7 eggs

Directions:

1. Add the ingredients into the bread machine as per the instructions of the manufacturer.
2. Set the program of your bread machine to BASIC and set the crust type to LIGHT.
3. Press START.
4. Once the loaf is ready, take the bucket out and let the loaf cool for 5 minutes.
5. Gently shake the bucket to remove the loaf.
6. Transfer to a cooling rack, slice, and serve.

Nutritional Content
Calories: 170; Carbs: 21g; Fat: 8g; Protein: 4.6g

Keto Sandwich Bread

Preparation Time: 5 minutes
Cooking Time: 1 hour
Servings: 12

Ingredients:
- 5 ml (1 tsp) apple cider vinegar
- 180 ml (¾ cup) water
- 60 ml (¼ cup) avocado oil
- 5 eggs
- 5 g (½ tsp) salt
- 5 g (1 tsp) baking soda
- 55 g (1.9 oz/½ cup) coconut flour
- 200 g (7.1 oz/2 cups+2 tbsp) almond flour

Directions:
1. Add all of the ingredients to your bread machine, carefully following the instructions of the manufacturer
2. Set the program of your bread machine to Basic/White Bread and set crust type to Medium. Press START
3. Wait until the cycle completes
4. Once the loaf is ready, take the bucket out and let the loaf cool for 5 minutes
5. Gently shake the bucket to remove the loaf
6. Transfer to a cooling rack, slice and serve

Nutritional Content
Calories: 200 g; Fat: 7 g; Carbs: 7 g; Protein: 16 g.

Almond Flour Lemon Bread

Preparation Time: 15 minutes
Cooking Time: 45 minutes
Servings: 16

Ingredients:

- 5 g (1 tsp) French herbs
- 5 ml (1 tsp) lemon juice
- 5 g (½ tsp) salt
- 5 g (1 tsp) cream of tartar
- 10 g (2 tsp) baking powder
- 60 g (2 oz/¼ cup) butter, melted
- 5 large eggs, divided
- 30 g (1 oz/¼ cup) coconut flour
- 145 g (5.1 oz/1½ cups) almond flour

Directions:

1. Add all of the ingredients to your bread machine, carefully following the instructions of the manufacturer
2. Set the program of your bread machine to Basic/White Bread and set crust type to Medium. Press START
3. Wait until the cycle completes
4. Once the loaf is ready, take the bucket out and let the loaf cool for 5 minutes
5. Gently shake the bucket to remove the loaf
6. Transfer to a cooling rack, slice and serve

Nutritional Content

Calories: 115; Fat: 9.9 g; Carbs: 3.3 g; Protein: 5.2 g.

Garlic, Herb and Cheese Bread

Preparation Time: 5 minutes
Cooking Time: 2 hours
Servings: 12

Ingredients:

- 120 g (4.2 oz/½ cup) ghee
- 6 eggs
- 190 g (6.7 oz/2 cups) almond flour
- 5 g (1 tsp) baking powder
- 5 g (½ tsp) xanthan gum
- 235 g (8.3 oz/1 cup) cheddar cheese, shredded
- 10 g (1 tbsp) garlic powder
- 5 g (1 tbsp) parsley
- 5 g (½ tbsp) oregano
- 5 g (½ tsp) salt

Directions:

1. Lightly beat eggs and ghee before pouring into bread machine pan.
2. Add the remaining ingredients to the pan.
3. Set the bread machine to gluten-free.
4. When the bread is done, remove the bread machine pan from the bread machine.
5. Let it cool slightly before transferring to a cooling rack.
6. You can store your bread for up to 5 days in the refrigerator.

Nutritional Content

Calories: 156; Carbs: 4 g; Fats: 13 g; Sugar: 4g; Protein: 5 g.

Cheesy Keto Sesame Bread

Preparation Time: 5 minutes
Cooking Time: 30 minutes
Servings: 8

Ingredients:
- 5 g (1 tsp) sesame seeds
- 5 g (1 tsp) baking powder
- 5g (½ tsp) salt
- 10 g (2 tsp) ground psyllium husk powder
- 95 g (3.4 oz/1 cup) almond flour
- 60 ml (4 tbsp) olive oil
- 200 g (7 oz) cream cheese
- 4 eggs
- 5 g (½ tsp) sea salt

Directions:
1. Add all of the ingredients to your bread machine, carefully following the instructions of the manufacturer
2. Set the program of your bread machine to Basic/White Bread and set crust type to Medium. Press START.
3. Wait until the cycle completes
4. Once the loaf is ready, take the bucket out and let the loaf cool for 5 minutes
5. Gently shake the bucket to remove the loaf
6. Transfer to a cooling rack, slice and serve

Nutritional Content
Calories: 282; Fat: 26 g; Carbs: 2 g; Protein: 7 g.

Chapter 5: Herbs and Spices Bread Recipes

Cajun Bread

Preparation Time: 10 minutes
Cooking Time: 2 hours 10 minutes
Servings: 14 slices

Ingredients:

- 120 ml (½ cup) water
- 4 onions, chopped
- 2 medium green bell pepper, chopped
- 2 garlic cloves, finely chopped
- 10 g (2 tsps.) soft butter
- 240 g (8.5 oz/2 cups) bread flour
- 10 g (1 tbsp) sugar
- 5 g (1 tsp) Cajun
- 5 g (½ tsp) salt
- 5 g (1 tsp) active dry yeast

Directions:

1. Add each ingredient to the bread machine in the order and at the temperature recommended by your bread machine manufacturer.
2. Close the lid, select the basic bread, medium crust setting on your bread machine, and press Start.
3. When the bread machine has finished baking, remove the bread and put it on a cooling rack.

Nutritional Content
Calories: 150; Carbs: 23 g; Fat: 4 g; Protein: 5 g.

Lavender Buttermilk Bread

Preparation Time: 10 minutes
Cooking Time: 3 hours
Servings: 8

Ingredients:
- 120 ml (½ cup) water
- 207 ml (⅞ cup) buttermilk
- 60 ml (¼ cup) olive oil
- 10 g (3 tbsp) fresh lavender leaves, finely chopped
- 5 g (1¼ tsp) lavender flowers
- 5 g Grated zest of 1 lemon
- 480 g (16.9oz/4 cups) bread flour
- 5 g (1 tsp) salt
- 10 g (2¾ tsp) bread machine yeast

Directions:
1. Add each ingredient to the bread machine in the order and at the temperature recommended by your bread machine manufacturer.
2. Close the lid, select the basic bread, medium crust setting on your bread machine, and press Start.
3. When the bread machine has finished baking, remove the bread and put it on a cooling rack.

Nutritional Content
Calories: 160; Carbs: 27 g; Fat: 5 g; Protein: 2 g.

Rosemary Bread

Preparation Time: 5 minutes
Cooking Time: 3 hours
Servings: 14 slices

Ingredients:
- 315 ml (1 1/3 cups) milk
- 60 g (2 oz/4 tbsp) butter
- 410 g (14.5/3 cups) bread flour
- 80 g (2.8 oz/1 cup) one-minute oatmeal
- 5 g (½ tsp) salt
- 25 g (6 tsp) white granulated sugar
- 5 g (1 tbsp) onion powder
- 5 g (1 tbsp) dried rosemary
- 5 g (1½ tsp) bread machine yeast

Directions:
1. Add each ingredient to the bread machine in the order and at the temperature recommended by your bread machine manufacturer.
2. Close the lid, select the basic bread, medium crust setting on your bread machine, and press Start.
3. After the bread machine has finished kneading, sprinkle some rosemary on top of the bread dough.
4. When the bread machine has finished baking, remove the bread and put it on a cooling rack.

Nutritional Content
Calories: 123; Carbs: 27 g; Fat: 3 g; Protein: 5 g

Chive Bread

Preparation Time: 10 minutes
Cooking Time: 3 hours
Servings: 14 slices

Ingredients:
- 160 ml (2/3 cup) milk at 25°C (80°F)
- 60 ml (¼ cup) water 25°C (80°F)
- 120 g (40 oz/¼ cup) sour cream
- 30 g (1 oz/2 tbsp) butter
- 5 g (1½ tsp) sugar
- 5 g (½ tsp) salt
- 360 g (12.7 oz/3 cups) bread flour
- 1 g (⅛ tsp) baking soda
- 5 g (¼ cup) minced chives
- 10 g (2¼ tsp) active dry yeast leaves

Directions:
1. Add each ingredient to the bread machine in the order and at the temperature recommended by your bread machine manufacturer.
2. Close the lid, select the basic bread, medium crust setting on your bread machine, and press Start.
3. When ready, put the bread on a cooling rack for about 20 minutes to cool.
4. Serve and enjoy.

Nutritional Content
Calories: 105; Carbs: 18 g; Fat: 2 g; Protein: 4 g.

Pumpkin Cinnamon Bread

Preparation Time: 10 minutes
Cooking Time: 3 hours
Servings: 14 slices

Ingredients:
- 100 g (3.5/1 cup) sugar
- 225 g (8 oz/1 cup) canned pumpkin
- 180 g (6 oz/1½ cups) all-purpose bread flour
- 80 ml (1/3 cup) vegetable oil
- 5 g (1 tsp) vanilla
- 2 eggs
- 5 g (¼ tsp) salt
- 5 g (1 tsp) ground cinnamon
- 10 g (2 tsp) baking powder
- 5 g (¼ tsp) ground nutmeg
- 1 g (⅛ tsp) ground cloves

Directions:
1. Add each ingredient to the bread machine in the order and at the temperature recommended by your bread machine manufacturer.
2. Close the lid, select the quick, medium crust setting on your bread machine, and press Start.
3. When ready, put the bread on a cooling rack for about 20 minutes to cool.
4. Serve and enjoy.

Nutritional Content
Calories: 140; Carbs: 39 g; Fat: 5 g; Protein: 3 g.

Cinnamon Raisin Bread

Preparation Time: 20 minutes
Cooking Time: 2 hours, 30 minutes
Servings: 7

Ingredients:
- 45 g (1.6 oz/3 tbsps.) butter
- 295 ml (1¼ cups) water
- 40 g (1.4 oz/ 3 tbsps.) brown sugar
- 5g (½ tsp) salt
- 10 g (2 tbsp) dry non-fat milk
- 390 g (13.8 oz/3¼ cups) bread flour
- 5 g (2 tsps.) dry active yeast
- 5 g (2 tsps.) 2 teaspoons cinnamon
- 160 g (5.6 oz/1 cup) raisins

Directions:
1. Add everything in the pan of your bread machine, except the raisins.
2. Process bread in your bread machine at the rapid, sweet, or timed cycle.
3. Add the raisins at the nut and fruit signal. You will get the signal between 30-40 minutes of the cycle, depending on the machine you are using.
4. Bake the bread. Set aside for cooling before serving.

Nutritional Content
Calories 221; Carbs: 36 g; Fat 8 g; Protein 10 g

Warm Spiced Pumpkin Bread

Preparation Time: 2 hours
Cooking Time: 15 minutes
Servings: 7

Ingredients:

- 5 g butter for greasing the bucket
- 360 g (12.6 oz/1½ cups) pumpkin purée
- 3 eggs, at room temperature
- 1 g (½ tsp) ground cinnamon
- 75 g (2.6 oz/ 1/3 cup) melted butter, cooled
- 200 g (7.1 oz/1 cup) sugar
- 5 g (½ tsp) baking soda
- 360 g (12.7 oz/3 cups) all-purpose flour
- 5 g (1½ tsp) baking powder
- 5 g (¼ tsp) ground ginger
- 5 g (¼ tsp) ground nutmeg
- 5 g (¼ tsp) salt
- 5 g (Pinch) ground cloves

Directions:

1. Lightly grease the bread bucket with butter.
2. Add the pumpkin, eggs, butter, and sugar.
3. Program the machine for Quick/Rapid bread and press Start.
4. Let the wet ingredients be mixed by the paddles until the first fast mixing cycle is finished, about 10 minutes into the cycle.
5. Stir together the flour, baking powder, cinnamon, baking soda, nutmeg, ginger, salt, and cloves until well blended.
6. Add the dry ingredients to the bucket when the second fast mixing cycle starts.
7. When the loaf is done, remove the bucket from the machine.
8. Let the loaf cool for 5 minutes.
9. Gently shake the bucket to remove the loaf and turn it out onto a rack to cool.

Nutritional Content
Calories: 251; Carbs: 43 g; Fat: 7 g; Protein: 5 g

Chapter 6: Gluten-Free Breads

Chia Seeds Bread

Preparation Time: 30 minutes
Cooking Time: 40 minutes
Servings: 6

Ingredients:
- 235 ml (1 cup) warm water
- 3 large organic eggs, room temperature
- 60 ml (¼ cup) olive oil
- 15 ml (1 tbsp) apple cider vinegar
- 170 g (6 oz/1 cup) gluten-free chia seeds, ground to flour
- 100 g (3.5 oz/1 cup) almond meal flour
- 95 g (3.4 oz/½ cup) potato starch
- 30 g (1 oz/¼ cup) coconut flour
- 100 g (3.5/¾ cup) millet flour
- 5 g (1 tbsp) xanthan gum
- 5 g (½ tsp) salt
- 25 g (0.9 oz/2 tbsp) sugar
- 15 g (3 tbsps.) nonfat dry milk
- 20 g (6 tsp) instant yeast

Directions:
1. Whisk wet ingredients together and add to the bread maker pan.
2. Whisk dry ingredients, except yeast, together and add on top of wet ingredients.
3. Make a well in the dry ingredients and add yeast.
4. Select Whole Wheat cycle, light crust color, and press Start.
5. Allow to cool completely before serving.

Nutritional Content

Cherry-Blueberry Loaf

Preparation Time: 10 minutes
Cooking Time: 3 hours
Servings: 6

Ingredients:
- 480 g (16.9 oz/4 cups) bread flour
- 55 g (1.9 oz/¼ cup) brown sugar
- 60 g (2 oz/ 1/3 cup) dried cherries, chopped
- 60 g (2 oz/ 1/3 cup) dried blueberries, chopped
- 5 g (2 tsp) yeast
- 5 g (½ tsp) salt
- 235 ml (1 cup) of water
- 30 ml (2 tbsps.) vegetable oil

Directions:
1. After pouring the water and oil into the bread pan, add the dry ingredients into the mix.
2. Press the "Basic" mode of the bread machine.
3. Choose either a light or medium crust color setting.
4. Once the cycles are done, transfer the bread to a wire rack.
5. Cooldown the bread completely before slicing.

Nutritional Content
Calories: 145; Carbs: 29g; Fat: 2g; Protein: 4g

Saltless White Bread

Preparation Time: 20 minutes
Cooking Time: 3 hours
Servings: 1 Pound Loaf

Ingredients:
- 120 ml (½ cup) Lukewarm water
- 5 g (1 tsp) Sugar
- 5 g (¾ tsp) Instant dry yeast
- 300 g (10.6 oz/2½ cups) White all-purpose flour
- 5 ml (½ tbsp) Extra-virgin olive oil
- ½ Egg white

Directions:
1. In a mixing bowl, combine the sugar and water. Stir until the sugar has dissolved and then add in the yeast.
2. Add the flour, water mixture, and oil to the bread maker.
3. Select the French loaf setting and medium crust function.
4. Five minutes into the cycle, add in the egg white and allow the bread cycle to continue.
5. When ready, turn the bread out onto a drying rack and allow it to cool, then serve.

Nutritional Content
Calories: 275.3; Fat: 3 g; Carbs: 52.9 g; Protein: 7.9 g

Gluten-Free Whole Grain Bread

Preparation Time: 2 hours
Cooking Time: 30 minutes
Servings: 6

Ingredients:

- 80 g (2.8 oz/ 2/3 cup) sorghum flour
- 60 g (2 oz/½ cup) buckwheat flour
- 60 g (2 oz/½ cup) millet flour
- 140 g (4.9 oz/¾ cup) potato starch
- 10 g (2¼ tsp) xanthan gum
- 5 g (¼ tsp) salt
- 180 g (6.3 oz/¾ cup) skim milk
- 120 ml (½ cup) water
- 5 g (1 tbsp) instant yeast
- 35 g (1.2 oz/5 tsp) agave nectar, separated
- 1 large egg, lightly beaten
- 60 ml (4 tbsp) extra virgin olive oil
- 5 ml (½ tsp) cider vinegar
- 5 g (1 tbsp) poppy seeds

Directions:

1. Whisk sorghum, buckwheat, millet, potato starch, xanthan gum, and sea salt in a bowl and set aside.
2. Combine milk and water in a glass measuring cup. Heat to between 110°F (43°C) and 120°F (49°C); add 2 teaspoons of agave nectar and yeast and stir to combine. Cover and set aside for a few minutes.
3. Combine the egg, olive oil, remaining agave, and vinegar in another mixing bowl; add yeast and milk mixture. Pour wet ingredients into the bottom of your bread maker.
4. Top with dry ingredients.
5. Select Gluten-Free cycle, light color crust, and press Start.
6. After second kneading cycle sprinkle with poppy seeds.
7. Remove pan from bread machine. Leave the loaf in the pan for about 5 minutes before cooling on a rack.

Nutritional Content
Calories: 130.3; Fat: 4 g; Carbs: 20 g; Protein: 3 g

Gluten-Free Brown Bread

Preparation Time: 2 hours
Cooking Time: 30 minutes
Servings: 6
Serves 12

Ingredients:

- 2 large eggs, lightly beaten
- 415 ml (1¾ cups) warm water
- 45 ml (3 tbsps.) canola oil
- 130 g (4.6 oz/1 cup) brown rice flour
- 65 g (2.3 oz/¾ cup) oat flour
- 40 g (1.4 oz/¼ cup) tapioca starch
- 240 g (8.5 oz/1¼ cups) potato starch
- 5 g (½ tsp) salt
- 25 g (0.9 oz/2 tbsp) brown sugar
- 15 g (2 tbsp) gluten-free flaxseed meal
- 55 g (1.9 oz/½ cup) nonfat dry milk powder
- 5 g (2½ tsp) xanthan gum
- 15 g (3 tbsp) psyllium, whole husks
- 10 g (2½ tsp) gluten-free yeast for bread machines

Directions:

1. Add the eggs, water and canola oil to the bread maker pan and stir until combined.
2. Whisk all of the dry ingredients except the yeast together in a large mixing bowl.
3. Add the dry ingredients on top of the wet ingredients.
4. Make a well in the center of the dry ingredients and add the yeast.
5. Set Gluten-Free cycle, medium crust color, and press Start.
6. When the bread is done, lay the pan on its side to cool before slicing to serve.

Nutritional Content

Raisin Bread

Preparation Time: 1 hour
Cooking Time: 25 minutes
Servings: 6

Ingredients:

- 175 ml (¾ cup) almond milk
- 15 g (2 tbsp) flax meal
- 90 ml (6 tbsp) warm water
- 5 ml (1 tsp) apple cider vinegar
- 30 g (1 oz/2 tbsp) butter
- 30 g (1 oz/1½ tbsp) honey
- 210 g (7.4 oz/1 2/3 cups) brown rice flour
- 30 g (1 oz/¼ cup) corn starch
- 20 g (2 tbsp) potato starch
- 5 g (1½ tsp) xanthan gum
- 5 g (1 tbsp) cinnamon
- 5 g (½ tsp) salt
- 1 g (1 tsp) active dry yeast
- 80 g (2.8 oz/½ cup) raisins

Directions:

1. Mix together flax and water and let stand for 5 minutes.
2. Combine dry ingredients in a separate bowl, except for yeast.
3. Add wet ingredients to the bread machine.
4. Add the dry mixture on top and make a well in the middle of the dry mixture.
5. Add the yeast to the well.
6. Set to Gluten Free, light crust color, and press Start.
7. After first kneading and rise cycle, add raisins.
8. Remove to a cooling rack when baked and let cool for 15 minutes before slicing.

Nutritional Content

Oat Bread

Preparation Time: 40 minutes
Cooking Time: 30 minutes
Servings: 6

Ingredients:
- 295 ml (1¼ cups) warm water
- 65 g (3 tbsp) honey
- 2 eggs
- 45 g (1.6 oz/3 tbsp) butter, melted
- 100 g (3.5 oz/1¼ cups) gluten-free oats
- 160 g (5.6 oz/1¼ cups) brown rice flour
- 95 g (3.5 oz/ ½ cup) potato starch
- 5 g (2 tsp) xanthan gum
- 10 g (1½ tsp) sugar
- 5 g (¾ tsp) salt
- 10 g (1½ tbsp) active dry yeast

Directions:
1. Add ingredients according to the manufacturer's instructions, except for yeast.
2. Make a well in the center of the dry ingredients and add the yeast.
3. Select Gluten-Free cycle, light crust color, and press Start.
4. Remove bread and allow the bread to cool on its side on a cooling rack for 20 minutes before slicing to serve.

Nutritional Content
Calories: 110; Carbs: 19g; Fat: 2g; Protein: 4g

Gluten-Free Chocolate Zucchini Bread

Preparation Time: 5 minutes
Cooking Time: 15 minutes
Servings: 12

Ingredients:

- 170 (6 oz/1½ cups) coconut flour
- 30 g (1 oz/¼ cup) unsweetened cocoa powder
- 100 g (3.5 oz/½ cup) erythritol
- 5 g (½ tsp) cinnamon
- 5 g (1 tsp) baking soda
- 5 g (1 tsp) baking powder
- 5 g (¼ tsp) salt
- 60 ml (¼ cup) coconut oil, melted
- 4 eggs
- 5 ml (1 tsp) vanilla
- 230 g (8.1 oz/2 cups) zucchini, shredded

Directions:

1. Shred the zucchini and use paper towels to drain excess water, set aside.
2. Lightly beat eggs with coconut oil then add to bread machine pan.
3. Add the remaining ingredients to the pan.
4. Set bread machine to gluten-free.
5. When the bread is done, remove the bread machine pan from the bread machine.
6. Let cool slightly before transferring to a cooling rack.

Nutritional Content
Calories 185; Carbs: 6 g; Fats 17 g; Protein 5 g

Cajun Veggie Loaf

Preparation Time: 15 minutes
Cooking Time: 15 minutes
Servings: 12

Ingredients:

- 120 ml (½ cup) water
- 2 onions, chopped
- 2 medium green bell peppers, chopped
- 5 g (2 tsp) garlic, chopped finely
- 9 g (2 tsp) ghee
- 190 g (6.7 oz/2 cups) almond flour
- 5 g (1 tbsp) inulin
- 5 g (1 tsp) Cajun seasoning
- 5 g (1 tsp) active dry yeast

Directions:

1. Add water and ghee to the bread machine pan.
2. Add in the remaining ingredients.
3. Set the bread machine to the basic setting.
4. When done, remove from the bread machine and allow cooling before slicing.
5. Let it cool slightly before transferring to a cooling rack.
6. You can store your bread for up to 5 days in the refrigerator.

Nutritional Content

Calories: 10; Carbs: 6 g; Protein: 4 g; Fat: 8 g.

Almond Butter Brownies

Preparation Time: 5 minutes
Cooking Time: 10 minutes
Servings: 14

Ingredients:
- 255 g (9 oz/1 cup) almond butter
- 10 g (2 tbsp) cocoa powder, un sweetened
- 120 ml (½ cup) erythritol
- 45 g (1.5 oz/¼ cup) dark chocolate chips, sugar-free
- 1 egg
- 45 ml (3 tbsps.) almond milk, unsweetened

Directions:
1. Beat egg and almond butter together in a mixing bowl.
2. Add in erythritol and cocoa powder.
3. If the mixture is too crumbly or dry, add in almond milk until you have a smooth consistency.
4. Fold in dark chocolate chips.
5. Pour mixture into bread machine pan.
6. Set bread machine to bake.
7. When done remove from bread machine and transfer to a cooling rack.
8. Cool completely before serving, you can store for up to 5 days in the refrigerator.

Nutritional Content
Calories: 141; Carbs: 3 g; Protein: 5g, Fat: 12 g.

Low Carb Flax Bread

Preparation Time: 10 minutes
Cooking Time: 24 minutes
Servings: 8

Ingredients:

- 200 g (7.1 oz) ground flax seeds
- 40 g (1.4 oz/½ cup) psyllium husk powder
- 5 g (1 tbsp) heating powder
- 100 g (3.5 oz/1½ cups) soy protein disengage
- 60 g (2.1 oz/¼ cup) granulated stevia
- 5 g (½ tsp) salt
- 7 egg whites
- 1 entire egg
- 50 g (3 tbsp) margarine
- 180 ml (¾ cup) water

Directions:

1. Add all of the ingredients to your bread machine, carefully following the instructions of the manufacturer
2. Set the program of your bread machine to Basic/White Bread and set crust type to Medium. Press START
3. Wait until the cycle completes
4. Once the loaf is ready, take the bucket out and let the loaf cool for 5 minutes
5. Gently shake the bucket to remove the loaf
6. Transfer to a cooling rack, slice and serve

Nutritional Content
Calories: 20, Carbs: 5g; Fat: 13 g; Protein: 10g

Bagels with Poppy Seeds

Preparation Time: 5 Minutes
Cooking Time: 25 Minutes
Servings: 8

Ingredients:
- 25 ml (1 cup) warm water
- 5 g (½ tsp) salt
- 25 g (0.9 oz/2 tbsps.) white sugar
- 360 g (12.8 oz/3 cups) bread flour
- 20 g 2 ¼ teaspoons active dry yeast
- 600 ml (2½ cup) boiling water
- 40 g (1.4 oz/3 tbsp.) white sugar
- 10 g (1 tbsp) cornmeal
- 1 egg white
- 36 g (1.2 oz/3 tbsp.) poppy seeds

Directions:
1. In the bread machine's pan, pour in the water, salt, sugar, flour, and yeast following the order of ingredients suggested by the manufacturer. Choose the Dough setting on the machine.
2. Once the machine has finished the whole cycle, place the dough on a clean surface covered with a little bit of flour; let it rest. While the dough is resting on the floured surface, put 3 quarts of water in a big pot and let it boil. Add in 3 tablespoons of sugar and mix.
3. Divide the dough evenly into nine portions and shape each into a small ball. Press down each dough ball until it is flat. Use your thumb to make a shack in the center of each flattened dough. Increase the hole's size in the center and smoothen out the dough around the hole area by spinning the dough on your thumb or finger. Use a clean cloth to cover the formed bagels and let it sit for 10 minutes.
4. Cover the bottom part of an ungreased baking sheet evenly with cornmeal. Place the bagels gently into the boiling water. Let it boil for 1 minute and flip it on the other side halfway through. Let the bagels drain quickly on a clean towel. Place the boiled bagels onto the prepared baking sheet. Coat the topmost of each bagel with egg white and top it off with your preferred toppings.
5. Put the bagels into the preheated 375°F (190°C) oven and bake for 20-25 minutes until it turns nice brown.

Nutritional Content
Calories: 50; Fat: 1.3; Carbs: 8.8; Protein: 1.4

Parmesan Italian Bread

Preparation Time: 16 minutes
Cooking Time: 15 minutes
Servings: 10

Ingredients:

- 355 ml (1 1/3 cup) warm water
- 30 ml (2 tbsps.) olive oil
- 2 cloves of garlic, crushed
- 5 g (1 tbsp) basil
- 5 g (1 tbsp) oregano
- 5g (1 tbsp) parsley
- 190 g (6.7 oz/2 cups) almond flour
- 5 g (1 tbsp) inulin
- 50 g (1.8 oz/½ cup) Parmesan cheese, grated
- 5 g(1 tsp) active dry yeast

Directions:

1. Pour all wet ingredients into the bread machine pan.
2. Add all dry ingredients to the pan.
3. Set the bread machine to French bread.
4. When the bread is done, remove the bread machine pan from the bread machine.
5. Let it cool slightly before transferring to a cooling rack.
6. You can store your bread for up to 7 days.

Nutritional Content
Calories: 150; Carbs: 14 g; Protein: 5 g; Fat: 5 g

Nisu Bread

Preparation Time: 10 minutes
Cooking Time: 2 hours
Servings: 8

Ingredients:
- 500 g (17.6 oz/4 cups) gluten-free self-rising flour
- 100 g (3.5 oz/½ cup) of sugar
- 40 g (1.4 oz/3 tbsp) butter
- 5 g (1 tsp) ground cardamom
- 5 g (1 teaspoon salt
- 1 egg
- 235 ml (1 cup) evaporated milk
- 60 ml (¼ cup) water

Directions:
1. Add the wet ingredients first to the bread pan before adding the dry ingredients.
2. Press the " Gluten-Free" mode and light crust setting on the bread machine.
3. Wait until every cycle is through.
4. Cooldown the bread completely.
5. Slice and serve.

Nutritional Content
Calories: 184; Carbs: 31g; Fat: 27g; Protein: 5g

Nutty Cinnamon Bread

Preparation Time: 10 minutes
Cooking Time: 2 hours
Servings: 8

Ingredients:

- 425 g (15 oz/3½ cups) gluten-free self-rising flour
- 65 g (2.3 oz/½ cup) pecans, chopped
- 60 g (2.1 oz/¼ cup) butter
- 40 g (1.4 oz/3 tbsp) brown sugar
- 15 g (0.5 oz/1½ tbsp) powdered milk
- 5 g (1 tsp) cinnamon
- 5 g (1 tsp) salt
- 295 ml (1¼ cups) water

Directions:

1. Pour the water first into the bread pan, and then add the dry ingredients.
2. Select the " Gluten-Free" mode of the bread machine with the light crust color setting.
3. Allow the machine to complete all cycles.
4. Remove the bread from the machine.
5. Cool down completely before slicing the bread.

Nutritional Content
Calories: 141; Carbs: 21g; Fat: 25g; Protein: 3g

Gluten-Free Crusty Boule Bread

Preparation Time: 15 minutes
Cooking Time: 3 hours
Servings: 12

Ingredients:
- 400 g (14.1 oz/3¼ cups) gluten-free flour mix
- 5 g (1 tsp) active dry yeast
- 5 g (½ tsp) kosher salt
- 10 g (1 tbsp) guar gum
- 315 ml (1 1/3 cups) warm water
- 2 large eggs, room temperature
- 30 ml (2 tbsp), plus 10 ml (2 tsp) olive oil
- 20 g (0.7 oz/1 tbsp) honey

Directions:
1. Combine all of the dry ingredients, do not include the yeast, in a large mixing bowl; set aside.
2. Mix the water, eggs, oil, and honey in a separate mixing bowl.
3. Pour the wet ingredients into the bread maker.
4. I am adding the dry ingredients on top of the wet ingredients.
5. Form a well in the center part of the dry ingredients and add the yeast.
6. Set to Gluten-Free setting and press Start.
7. Remove baked bread and allow it to cool completely. Hollow out and fill with soup or dip to use as a boule or slice for serving.

Nutritional Content
Calories: 480; Fat: 3.2 g; Carbs: 103.9 g; Protein: 2.4 g

Conclusion

If this cookbook has sparked joy in your kitchen and inspired delightful meals, we kindly ask for your help. Your reviews and feedback are the lifeblood of our business. Each review brings a smile to our faces and encourages us to continue creating exceptional cookbooks.

If you have a moment, we would be immensely grateful if you could leave a review online. Your words have the power to guide others towards new culinary adventures.

Furthermore, should you encounter any concerns or have any feedback, please reach out to us at divinecookingbooks@gmail.com We value your thoughts and opinions as we strive to improve our offerings and provide you with the best possible experience.

Printed in Great Britain
by Amazon